Editorial Project Manager
Paul Gardner

Editor
Jodi L. McClay, M.A.

Editor in Chief
Sharon Coan, M.S. Ed.

Art Director
Elayne Roberts

Art Coordinator
Cheri Macoubrie Wilson

Production Manager
Phil Garcia

Imaging
Ralph Olmedo, Jr.

Trademarks
Trademarked names and graphics appear throughout this book. Instead of listing every firm and entity which owns the trademarks or inserting a trademark symbol with each mention of a trademarked name, the publisher avers that it is using the names and graphics only for editorial purposes and to the benefit of the trademarked owner with no intention of infringing upon that trademark.

Publishers
Rachelle Cracchiolo, M.S. Ed.
Mary Dupuy Smith, M.S. Ed.

The Print Shop®: Simple Projects

Authors

Marsha Lifter, M.A. and Marian E. Adams

Teacher Created Materials, Inc.
6421 Industry Way
Westminster, CA 92683
www.teachercreated.com

©1999 Teacher Created Materials, Inc.
Reprinted, 2000
Made in U.S.A.
ISBN-1-57690-414-8

Table of Contents

Introduction

In your classroom or computer lab software collection is one of the most versatile computer programs ever written, *The Print Shop*. Your students can use the many project choices to create everything from banners to newspapers. *Simple Projects for The Print Shop* is divided into two distinct sections for student use:

- Student print projects
- Interactive templates

The student projects are written so that students can follow the directions and produce complete projects. Along the way they will undoubtedly add their own creative touches. We didn't label the projects as to grade level because there is such a variance today in the classroom. Review the project and assign students to the ones that are appropriate.

The templates are designed so that students can interact with the material already on the template and by adding material or relocating material on the screen, print out a unique project. It is our hope that students will learn more about using *The Print Shop* through manipulation of the templates. The templates are divided into Primary and Middle/Upper grade level because of the subject matter. For each template there are specific directions. Duplicate the directions and place them next to the computer. What a sneaky way to show students that they must read carefully to get all the directions correct!

It might be fun for you as the teacher to design your own templates for the students to use.

The Print Shop for Terrified Teachers, published by Teacher Created Materials, is also available for you to use as a tutorial for yourself and your students.

We hope that you enjoy *The Print Shop: Simple Projects*.

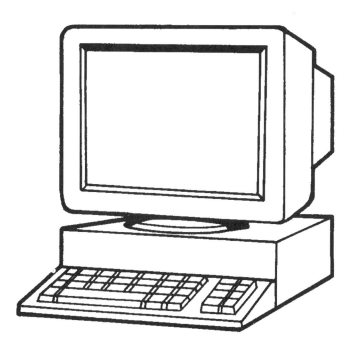

Special Notes For Windows Users

The Print Shop series of programs is published in both Macintosh and Windows versions. The directions in *The Print Shop: Simple Projects* were written for use on both. Basically, the directions in this book will work on a Windows machine with a few small additions. There are also some features unique to the Windows version. These will be marked with an asterisk *.

Windows: Starting New Projects

When you open a new project from the Select a Project dialog box, you are given two choices:

- Customize a Ready Made
- Start from Scratch

The Customize a Ready Made selection presents a layout with graphics that can be modified to suit your needs. The Start from Scratch option presents a blank page to create layouts and graphics.

Spell Check, Thesaurus, and Quotes and Verses

*Spell Check, Thesaurus, and Quotes and Verses are options which can be accessed from the File menu when you are using the Text Block.

Spell Check: Click Spell Check to check the entire contents of an Edit dialog box for misspelled or unfamiliar words. If an unfamiliar word is found:

- Replace With field–you can select a word from the Alternatives list to place in this field.
- Alternatives field–displays a list of suggested alternate words.
- Not Found field–displays the word not found.
- Ignore–ignores a word and continues spell checking the rest of the text.
- Replace–click to accept the word in the Replace With field.
- Add–adds a word to the Spell Check dictionary.

*Thesaurus: Search for synonyms for a currently highlighted word from within the Edit Text Block, Edit Word Balloon, or Edit Headline Text dialog boxes:

- Searched For field–displays the word being searched for in the thesaurus.
- Meanings field–displays a list of the meanings for the word being searched for.
- Replace With Synonym field–type a word or select a word from the Meanings list to replace the word in the Searched For field.
- Search–finds the synonym for the word displayed in the Replace With Synonym field.
- Previous–displays the previously searched for word.
- Replace–replaces the word in the Searched For field with the contents of the Replaced With Synonym field and closes the Thesaurus dialog box.

*Quotes and Verses Browser: Over 1,000 quotes and verses that can be incorporated into projects exist in the Windows version. In Edit Text or Edit Word Balloon Text dialog box, click on the Quotes and Verses button to add poetry, proverbs, humor, holiday greetings, and birthday facts to projects.

- Search button–searches for specific quotes and verses based on a keyword or keywords.
- Keywords field–type in keywords.
- Add Project Text button–adds text from the project to the Keywords field.
- Category Keywords button–takes you to the Keywords dialog box where you can choose from a list of search subjects.
- Search Preferences button–search for all words in the Keywords box individually or search for all words as they appear together.

Online Greeting Cards and the Internet Connection

You can create a unique online greeting with text and graphics and send it to someone over the Internet. Your greeting appears as an attachment in the e-mail of the person receiving the message. You must be connected to the Internet in order to send the greeting, and the recipient must be able to view JPEG image files.

In addition, Brøderbund provides registered *The Print Shop* users with technical support and lots of free graphics at their *The Print Shop* Connection Web site. You can access it at

http://www.printshop.com/

The Print Shop Idea Guide

There are three different graphic project themes in the Idea Guide: Party Ideas, Gift Ideas, and Holiday Ideas.

When you select one of these project themes, you are presented with four different projects having that theme:

- Party Ideas, Invitation, Table Runner, Place Card, and Game Poster.
- Gift Ideas, Gift Label, Gift Certificate, Money Envelope, and Recipe Card.
- Holiday Ideas, Greeting Card, Ornament, Paper Chain, and Count Down (a calendar).

The Idea Guide is stored on *The Print Shop Ensemble III* CD. To open the *Ensemble* Idea Guide in Windows 95:

- Insert the CD into you CD-ROM drive.
- Click start.
- Point to Programs—*The Print Shop*.
- Click *Ensemble* Idea Guide Icon.

The step-by-step instructions for each of these project ideas are presented using verbal instructions and animation. To print a copy of the instructions:

- Click How To (the *Ensemble* Idea Guide Help section opens with the project areas listed).
- Click Party Ideas.
- Click Invitation.
- Click File menu.
- Select Print Topic.

The instructions for the party invitation are printed.

The Tools and the Tool Palette

Teacher Note: Duplicate the following pages, glue them onto file folders, laminate them, and display them in the computer area for student reference.

The Tools and the Tool Palette *(cont.)*

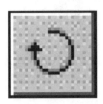

Rotate Tool

The Rotate Tool lets you rotate objects that have been selected. Click on a corner of the selected object and drag in either a clockwise or counterclockwise direction until the object is in the position in which you want it. If you want to rotate the object by a specific number of degrees, you can do it by selecting rotate from the Object menu and typing or selecting the specific rotation that you want.

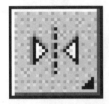

Flip Tool

The Flip Tool lets you flip a selected graphic object (except borders and mini-borders) horizontally, vertically, or both. When you select this tool, a menu appears. Choose Horizontal, Vertical, or Both. You can also flip an object by selecting Flip from the Object menu.

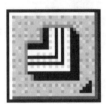

Frame Tool

The Frame Tool lets you place a frame around a selected object. When you select this tool, a menu appears. The choices are None, Thin Line, Thick Line, Double Line, or Drop Shadow. The current setting of the selected object is shown by a check mark. If a number of objects with different frame settings are selected, no check mark will appear. You can also frame an object by selecting Frame from the Object menu.

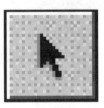

Pointer Tool

The Pointer Tool lets you select, move, and resize objects. To select an object, click on it. Handles appear at the corners of the object. This tells you that the object is selected.

To select additional objects, hold down the shift key while you click on the additional objects. You can change the size of the selected object by holding the mouse arrow down on one of the handles and moving the handle in or out to change the size. You move the object by holding down the mouse arrow in the center and moving the object to where you want it placed. Borders and backdrops cannot be resized.

Text Tool

The Text Tool lets you create text blocks, enter text, and select text to edit. To create a new text block, put the text cursor where you want the upper-left corner of the text block to be placed and drag diagonally to create a text box. You can now enter text in the block. If you want to change the font, size, style, justification, and/or placement, highlight the text and use the Text menu to make the changes. To change the color of the text, use the Color Bar on the Tool Palette.

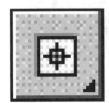

New Object Tool

The New Object Tool lets you add new objects to your projects such as:

- Square Graphic
- Row Graphic
- Column Graphic

- Text Block
- Headline
- Horizontal Ruled Line

- Vertical ruled Line
- Mini Border
- Border

The Tools and the Tool Palette *(cont.)*

Hold down your mouse arrow on the New Object Tool and move your mouse to the choice you want to select. Release the mouse button and the placeholder for the choice appears on your screen. Move the placeholder by clicking and dragging it to where you want it to be placed. Change the size by clicking and dragging one of the handles. To select a graphic or enter text, double-click on the placeholder.

Hand Tool

The Hand Tool lets you move your project around within the window. To use the Hand Tool, put the hand on your project and drag.

View Tool

The View Tool lets you change your view of the project. Select this tool and a menu will appear:

- Zoom In
- Zoom Out
- Fit in Window—the default for most projects, shows your project in a size that fits in the document window of your monitor
- Actual Size—shows the project at the size it is when printed out
- 25%—one quarter actual size
- 50%—one half actual size
- 150%—one and a half times actual size
- 200%—twice actual size

Delete Tool

The Delete Tool lets you delete a selected object. If you change your mind and want the deleted object back, select Undo from the Edit menu.

Color Control Panel

You can choose colors for various parts of the design by choosing items in the Color Control Panel. Click on the object you want to color using the Pointer Tool. Click on the Item Selector and choose an area to color from the menu that appears:

- Object (or Text)
- Behind the Object (or Text)
- Frame
- Backdrop
- Page

The current color for the selected location is shown in the Color Bar. Multi-colored objects are represented by three color splashes or the words "multi-colored." If the multi-colored objects are selected, they cannot be changed. If the item selected can be colored, click on the Color Bar and move to the color that you want to choose.

Alliterative Stories

This Project:

Alliteration is the use or repetition of a succession of words with the same initial letter or sound, as in "The river running round the rock." In this project you will design a page illustrating an alliterative sentence. This project example is for the letter M.

1. Open Sign from the Project Menu and then choose Blank Page and then No Layout from the Layout menu.

2. The first thing to do is place your letter at the top of the page. Select Object from the Tool Palette and choose Square Graphic. Put the placeholder in the upper left-hand side of the screen.

3. Double-click on the Square Graphic placeholder and search the graphics libraries for an alphabet. When you find an alphabet, choose the letter for your alliteration story.

4. Write the alliterative sentence at the bottom of the page. Select the Text tool "T" from the Tool Palette and click and drag a text box at the bottom of the page. You could also choose Object, Add, and Text from the menu bar and position your text box at the bottom of the page. Enlarge, if necessary, by pulling on one of the handles surrounding the text box.

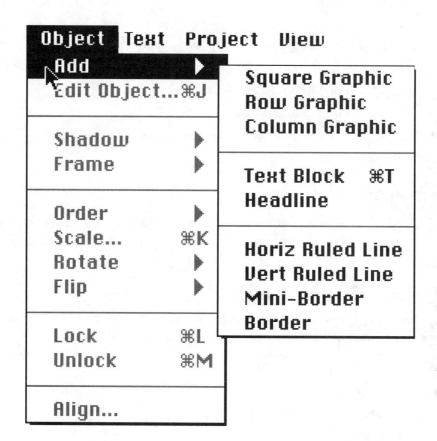

Alliterative Stories *(cont.)*

If you need to change your text after you have written it, double-click on the text and you are taken to the Edit Text dialog box where you can make changes.

5. After the sentence is written, illustrate it by selecting graphics and placing them on the screen. Select Object and then Square Graphic from the Tool Palette. Place the Square Graphic placeholder where you want it and double-click on it. Now search through the graphics to find one that illustrates a part of your sentence.

6. Choose a border for your page. Select Object and then Border from the Tool Palette or select Object, Add, and Border from the menu bar. Double-click on the grey border and select an appropriate border that adds to the design of your page.

7. When you are finished, select Print from the File menu.

What Else Can I Do?

• Make pages for many other letters of the alphabet and compile them into a classroom book.

• Write alliterative phrases instead of sentences. The phrases can consist of two or three adjectives and a noun. Examples: blue beaked birds, pretty perky pandas, Tommy takes toads, elephants eat eggs.

• Create and print some simple alliterative pages to compile into a book to give to the lower grades.

Pandas, penguins, pelicans and polar bears play ping pong.

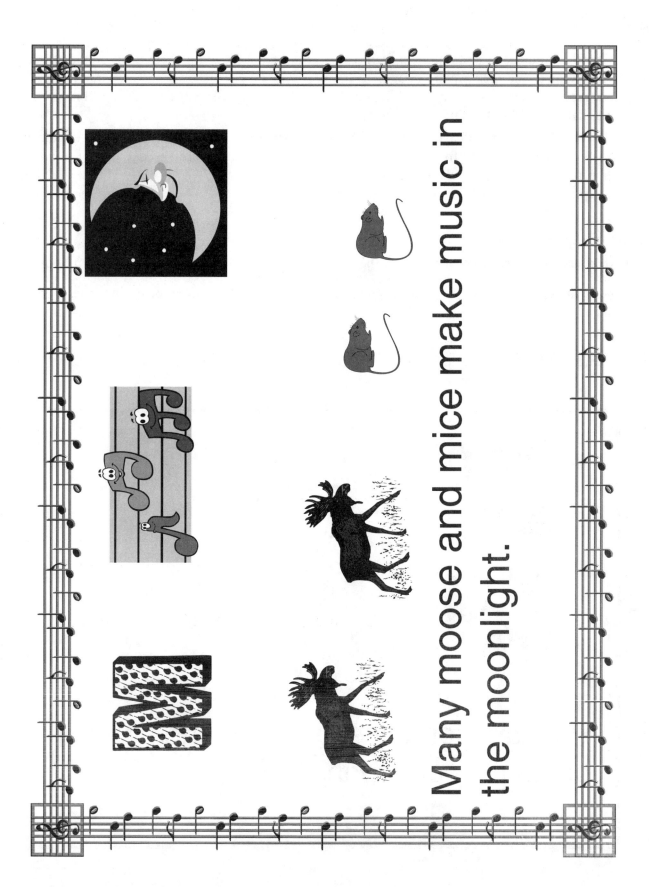

Many moose and mice make music in the moonlight.

Making Fun Banners

This Project:

Making banners to display in the classroom and for personal use is a fun way to highlight classroom events, personal events, and even historical events. In this project you will be making a banner for a special day.

1. Select Banner from the Project Menu.
2. On the next screen choose Horizontal or Vertical orientation. For this particular project we chose the Horizontal orientation.
3. On the next screen, choose a Backdrop or No Backdrop and click OK. If you choose a backdrop, the text on your banner will be placed with a background.
4. On the following screen choose the layout you want. Most of the layouts provide an area for text and areas for square graphics. For this example we choose Banner #1 for the layout. You can add more graphics to the banner if you want.
5. Click on the explanation mark and you are taken to the Banner Text screen. On this screen you write your text and modify it. You can change Font, Shape, Size, Justification, and Color.

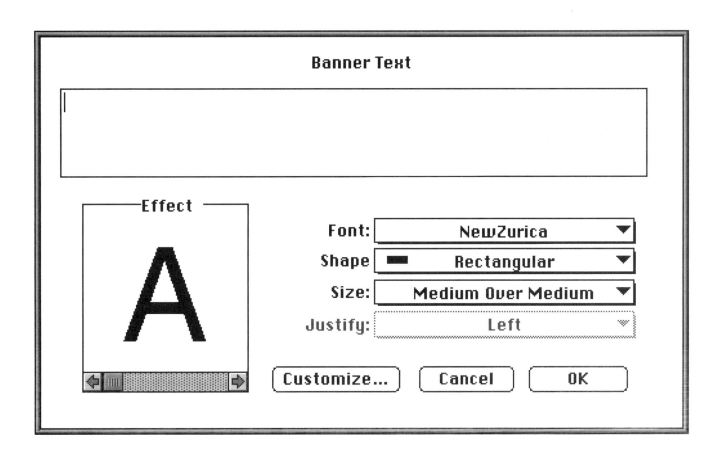

6. After you click OK and place the text, you can still change it. Double-click on it and you are then returned to the Banner Text screen where you can make changes.

7. You can use Square Graphic from Object in the Tool Palette to add more graphics. You might want to try using the Row Graphic for an interesting effect. Remember the graphics can be made smaller by moving the handles around the graphic.

8. If your layout has a grey edge, you can easily add a border. Double-click on the grey area and choose a border from the list presented. If your layout does not have a grey border, you can still add one to the banner. Select Border from the Object menu in the Tool Palette and choose a border for your banner.

9. Save and print your banner.

What Else Can I Do?

- Make a banner to announce a book report. This would be a good addition to an oral book report.
- Help decorate your classroom by making banners to label various bulletin boards.

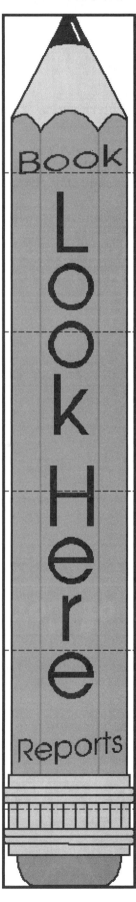

Designing Calendars

This Project:

In this project you will make a calendar for your own use. You will choose the month that you want and add appropriate events and graphics.

1. Select Calendar from the main project screen and then choose Monthly from the screen. Select Wide from the Calendar Orientation screen.

2. From the next screen select the year and month for the calendar. Click OK.

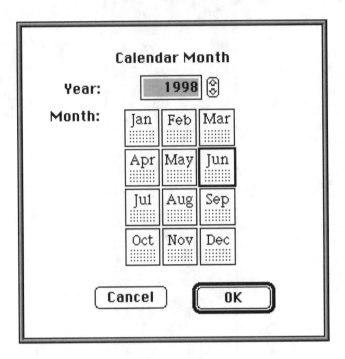

3. Select Blank Page and click OK. From the next screen you make a choice for a layout. The layout is where the text and the graphics will be placed. For this particular project Calendar 6 was selected.

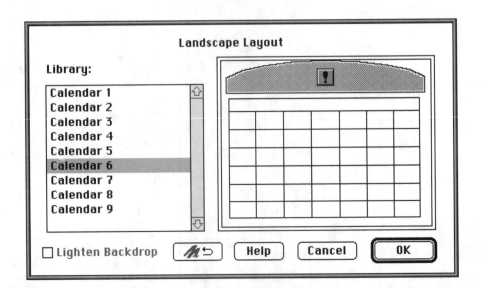

4. You see on the screen October 1998 in black and a blank calendar. Let's change the word October to another color. Double-click on the word and you see a dialog box on the screen. At the bottom of the box is a button marked Customize. Click on that button and the next screen shows another dialog box. Hold down the arrow in the middle rectangle of the Color selection area. Move your mouse arrow to the color you want and click OK. Click OK again and October is now in a different color.

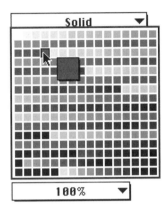

5. To mark Halloween, double-click in the date box Oct. 31. You are now in the Edit Calendar Day dialog box. Click on the Edit Text button. You are now on the Edit Text dialog box. Type in Halloween. You can also choose color by holding down the Color arrow and choosing a color. You can also change size by holding down the Size arrow. Click OK. Click OK again and you are on the screen with the calendar.

6. To add a graphic to the date, double-click on the date and choose Select Graphic from the dialog box. From the list of graphics presented, choose one that is good for a Halloween theme. If there are not any that are appropriate, select Change Libraries. Search the libraries for a Halloween graphic and when you find one, double-click to place it. Holiday Collection 4 has many Halloween graphics.

7. Now you can add the dates that are important to you. On which date is your book report due? Is there a ball game or other event you want to note?

What Else Can I Do?

- Make a calendar for February with the president's birthdays listed.
- Make a weekly calendar with all your activities listed.
- Make a blank calendar as a gift for someone. For this one, choose a background.

2000

January

S	M	T	W	T	F	S
						1
2	3	4	5	6	7	8
9	10	11	12	13	14	15
16	17	18	19	20	21	22
23	24	25	26	27	28	29
30	31					

February

S	M	T	W	T	F	S
		1	2	3	4	5
6	7	8	9	10	11	12
13	14	15	16	17	18	19
20	21	22	23	24	25	26
27	28	29				

March

S	M	T	W	T	F	S
			1	2	3	4
5	6	7	8	9	10	11
12	13	14	15	16	17	18
19	20	21	22	23	24	25
26	27	28	29	30	31	

April

S	M	T	W	T	F	S
						1
2	3	4	5	6	7	8
9	10	11	12	13	14	15
16	17	18	19	20	21	22
23	24	25	26	27	28	29
30						

May

S	M	T	W	T	F	S
	1	2	3	4	5	6
7	8	9	10	11	12	13
14	15	16	17	18	19	20
21	22	23	24	25	26	27
28	29	30	31			

June

S	M	T	W	T	F	S
				1	2	3
4	5	6	7	8	9	10
11	12	13	14	15	16	17
18	19	20	21	22	23	24
25	26	27	28	29	30	

July

S	M	T	W	T	F	S
						1
2	3	4	5	6	7	8
9	10	11	12	13	14	15
16	17	18	19	20	21	22
23	24	25	26	27	28	29
30	31					

August

S	M	T	W	T	F	S
		1	2	3	4	5
6	7	8	9	10	11	12
13	14	15	16	17	18	19
20	21	22	23	24	25	26
27	28	29	30	31		

September

S	M	T	W	T	F	S
					1	2
3	4	5	6	7	8	9
10	11	12	13	14	15	16
17	18	19	20	21	22	23
24	25	26	27	28	29	30

October

S	M	T	W	T	F	S
1	2	3	4	5	6	7
8	9	10	11	12	13	14
15	16	17	18	19	20	21
22	23	24	25	26	27	28
29	30	31				

November

S	M	T	W	T	F	S
			1	2	3	4
5	6	7	8	9	10	11
12	13	14	15	16	17	18
19	20	21	22	23	24	25
26	27	28	29	30		

December

S	M	T	W	T	F	S
					1	2
3	4	5	6	7	8	9
10	11	12	13	14	15	16
17	18	19	20	21	22	23
24	25	26	27	28	29	30
31						

Week of May 18, 1998

My Calendar

Monday 18	Copy Spelling Words	
Tuesday 19	Bring lunch money	
Wednesday 20	Return library books	
Thursday 21	Computer Class	
Friday 22	Book report due	
Saturday 23	Soccer game	
Sunday 24	Visit Grandma and Grandpa	

My Own Deck of Cards

This Project:

Using the business card option in *The Print Shop* you can easily create your own flash cards or even playing cards. Make these for games or create your own cards to practice math facts or parts of speech.

1. Open the Business Card Project from the main menu. Choose the Wide Orientation and click OK.

2. Choose a Backdrop design that you like from the choices on the Backdrop screen.

3. On the next screen choose the layout or the way the card is designed. For this project, choose a layout and press OK.

4. On the next screen you can create your project. There are spaces for text among the graphics.

5. To write the test, double-click on the Text placeholder and key in your text. You might want to key in your name since this is your deck of cards.

6. If the size of the font is too large, highlight it and choose the Size option from the Text menu on the menu bar. Select a smaller size and then write your text.

7. To make the playing card more elaborate, add a border for the text. Select the Object icon from the tool Palette and choose Border. You now have a greyed-out area around the page. Double-click on the grey area and choose a border for text on the screen.

8. When you are ready to print, select Print from the File menu and print your work.

9. Ask your teacher if you can use a heavier paper for these cards. Cardstock is a heavier weight that works well in the printer. After the cards are printed, cut them apart carefully.

10. Now turn the cards over and add the numbers and suits to make a deck of playing cards.

11. If you are making flash cards, after your cards are printed and cut apart, write a multiplication problem on the back. Continue writing the problems, one to a card, and use them to study when you are finished.

What Else Can I Do?

- Make cards with a holiday theme to give as presents.

- Use your study cards to learn your spelling words. Ask your teacher to laminate the cards and then you can change the study part of the card whenever needed.

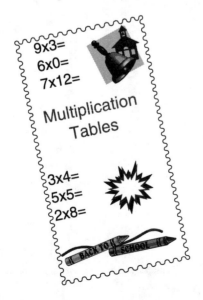

My Own Deck of Cards *(cont.)*

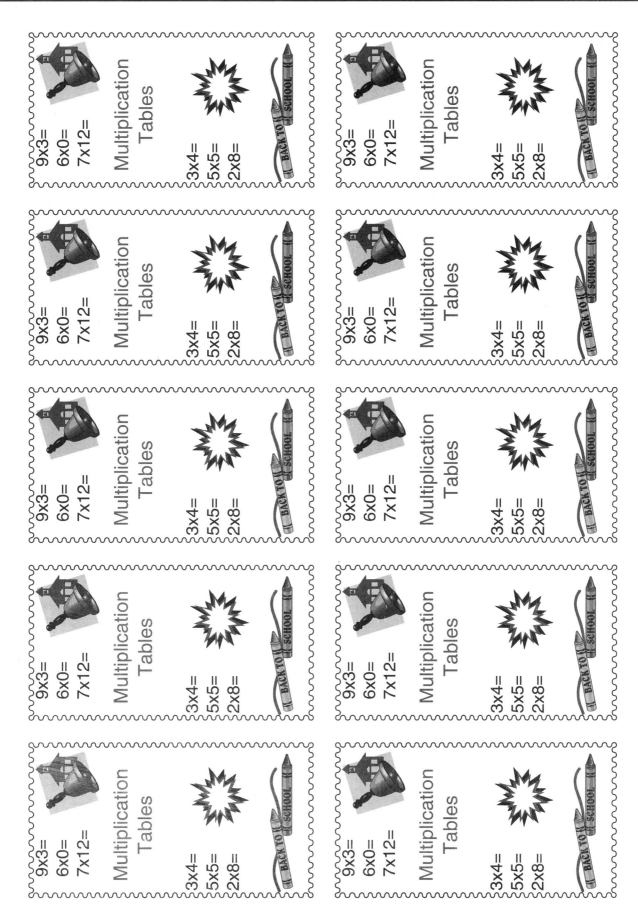

9x3=
6x0=
7x12=

Multiplication Tables

3x4=
5x5=
2x8=

9x3=
6x0=
7x12=

Multiplication Tables

3x4=
5x5=
2x8=

9x3=
6x0=
7x12=

Multiplication Tables

3x4=
5x5=
2x8=

9x3=
6x0=
7x12=

Multiplication Tables

3x4=
5x5=
2x8=

9x3=
6x0=
7x12=

Multiplication Tables

3x4=
5x5=
2x8=

9x3=
6x0=
7x12=

Multiplication Tables

3x4=
5x5=
2x8=

9x3=
6x0=
7x12=

Multiplication Tables

3x4=
5x5=
2x8=

9x3=
6x0=
7x12=

Multiplication Tables

3x4=
5x5=
2x8=

9x3=
6x0=
7x12=

Multiplication Tables

3x4=
5x5=
2x8=

9x3=
6x0=
7x12=

Multiplication Tables

3x4=
5x5=
2x8=

Solve It!

This Project:

You can create your own math book with problems for your friends and family to solve. Using *The Print Shop* and a printer, all you have to do is design the page, use some graphics, and print it. The graphics that are available will inspire you in your problem creation. First write down your problem on a piece of paper and look through the graphics available. Sketch how you would like the page to look. By preparing before you use the computer your time on the computer is much more productive.

1. Open the sign project from the main menu and choose Tall Orientation.

2. Choose a Blank Page from the next menu. Choose No Layout and click OK. On the screen is a blank page ready for your input.

3. Sometimes it is best to place the graphics first so that you can incorporate the text so that it looks like the graphics and text are interwoven.

4. Select Object from the Tool Palette and choose Square Graphic. Move the graphic placeholder to a place on the page where it will balance the text. Double-click on the Placeholder and choose your graphic. If you need more choice of graphics, click on More Libraries and choose from there.

   If you choose a graphic that really doesn't work, click on it once to get the handles and press Delete. Choose another graphic by following the directions in this section.

5. To place and write your text, select the Text tool from the Object Menu and click and drag in the area where you want the text. Type in your text. Remember that you can change your font and font size by highlighting the text and choosing new font and size from the Text menu on the menu bar.

6. You can also change the size of the text box by clicking on the Pointer Tool in the Tool Palette and then clicking on the text box. Now handles appear around the text box. Put your mouse arrow on one of the handles and drag it in or out depending on what size box you want.

7. Add more graphics and text to your page to complete your problem.

8. Now add a border to make your page graphically attractive. Select the Object Tool from the Tool Palette and choose Border. You now have a greyed-out area around the page. Double-click on the grey area and choose a border.

9. To create a section on your page for working out or illustrating the problem, you can add a small outlined square section. Select Object and choose Mini-border and place it on the page.

10. To print your page, select Print from the File menu. If you are making a problem for younger children, you might want to print in a 2x2 inch size.

What Else Can I Do?

- Make one math problem page for each operation that you have studied. Make a page with an addition problem, a page with a subtraction problem, a page with a multiplication problem, and a page with a division problem.

- Make a page where the solver has to illustrate the problem. In this case be sure to have a large Mini-border area.

Natalie's Birthday

Natalie invited 10 friends to her birthday party. Her mother cut the cake into 10 pieces. Well, there was a problem: each guest wanted two pieces of cake. How could Natalie's mother solve this problem?

Take Me Out To The Ballgame!

Stephens Elementary School's baseball teams were in a tournament with Locke Elementary. The winners of the tournament were going to the state playoffs. 27 students at Stephens had signed up to play. Since there are only 9 players on a team, how many teams will be formed?

Show the problem.

Locke School had 36 students who wanted to play. How many teams will they field?

Making Certificates

This Project:

It's really easy to create and print professional-looking certificates using *The Print Shop*. You can make certificates for your friends and family members and also make historically based certificates to accompany reports and presentations. For this example you will make a ready-made certificate for James Audubon.

Using the Ready Made Certificate Option:

1. Open Certificates from the Project screen. If you are using a Macintosh, you might need to open *The Print Shop Companion* and then open Certificate.

2. Select the orientation you want and then click on Ready Made. Now you see a long list of certificates. Select one that fits the theme of the certificate you want to make. For this example we chose Natural in order to make a certificate for James Audubon, recognizing the good work he did in identifying birds.

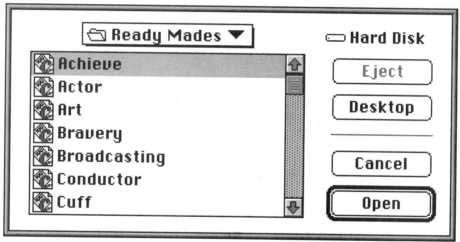

3. On the screen is a ready-made certificate which you need only to customize for your purpose.

4. Double-click on the name listed on the certificate and this takes you to a Headline Text dialog box. Highlight the name and press the delete key. Type in the name James Audubon. Click OK. Now the name appears on the screen.

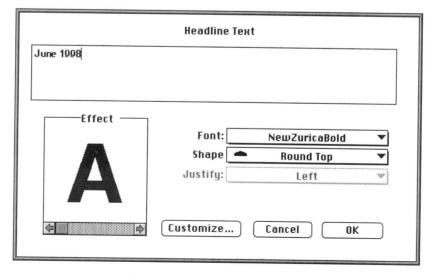

Making Certificates *(cont.)*

5. To add your own text under the name, double-click on the existing text and highlight. Key in the words for the text. For this example, we wrote For Teaching Us About Birds.

6. Now to change the signature names. To edit the signature, double-click in the signature area, and you are presented with an Edit signature dialog box. The box is divided into two areas; on the left is where you key in the signature. You can also change the color, size and justification by selecting choices on the left. To edit the signature on the right, double-click on the right signature and you go to the Edit Signature screen where you can make the changes. Click OK when you are finished and look how the signatures have changed.

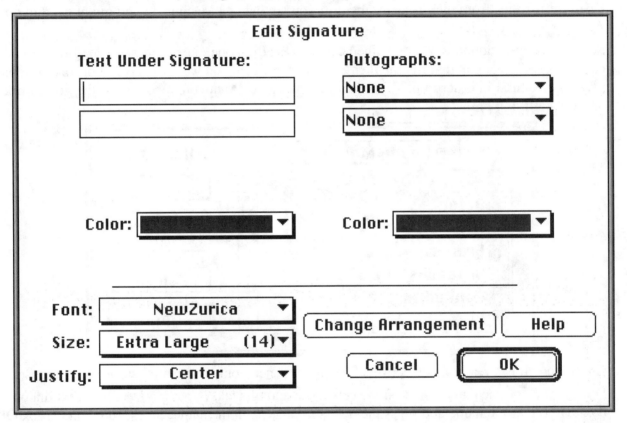

7. The border and the seal are appropriate for this award, so let's just leave them as they are.

8. Print your award by selecting File and then Print.

Making a Certificate from Scratch

1. Open Certificate project from the Project Menu. Macintosh users open *The Print Shop* and then *Print Shop Companion.* Select Certificate. For this example we are making a certificate for Sally Ride, who was the first woman in space.

2. Select either Wide or Tall orientation from the Orientation screen.

3. Select Blank Page and click on OK.

4. This next screen is the layout screen where you can choose how your certificate is going to look. Click on a layout to preview it in the preview box. Keep clicking on various layouts until you find one that suits you. For this example we used Layout 36. Click OK. It has a headline, text area, signature area, and seal area. You will be able to personalize the certificate to meet your needs.

5. Click on the Headline area first. The next screen is where you write your headline text and choose the font, color, and shape of the headline. Key in the name of the award. If you want to change the color of the lettering, click on Customize. On this screen you can select color, font, and style. Click OK when you are satisfied.

6. Now click on the Text placeholder and enter the name of the certificate recipient.

7. Click on the seal at the right of the screen and you are taken to the Seal dialog box. Here you can choose the center and the outer edge that you want.

8. To edit the signature, double-click on it and key in the signature you want.

9. Print your certificate.

Making Certificates *(cont.)*

What Else Can I Do?

- Make awards for friends in the class who have accomplished something unique.
- Make humorous awards for historical figures. You might want to include these awards in reports that you are writing and/or presenting.
- See what fun historical certificates you can make for these people.

    Alexander Graham Bell: invented the telephone

    Susan B. Anthony: worked to give women the right to vote

    Vincent Van Gogh: impressionist artist

    Sir Arthur Conan Doyle: writer of the Sherlock Holmes series

    Paul Bunyan: legendary folk hero, larger than life

    P.T. Barnum: made the circus popular

    Neil Armstrong: first man to walk on the moon

    Francis Scott Key: writer of the poem that became "The Star Spangled Banner"

    Jane Addams: worked for social reforms

    Washington Irving: wrote *The Legend of Sleepy Hollow*

    Benjamin Franklin: organized the postal system; invented the rocking chair and Franklin stove; discovered electricity

Woman in Space

1st

Sally Ride

Neal Armstrong

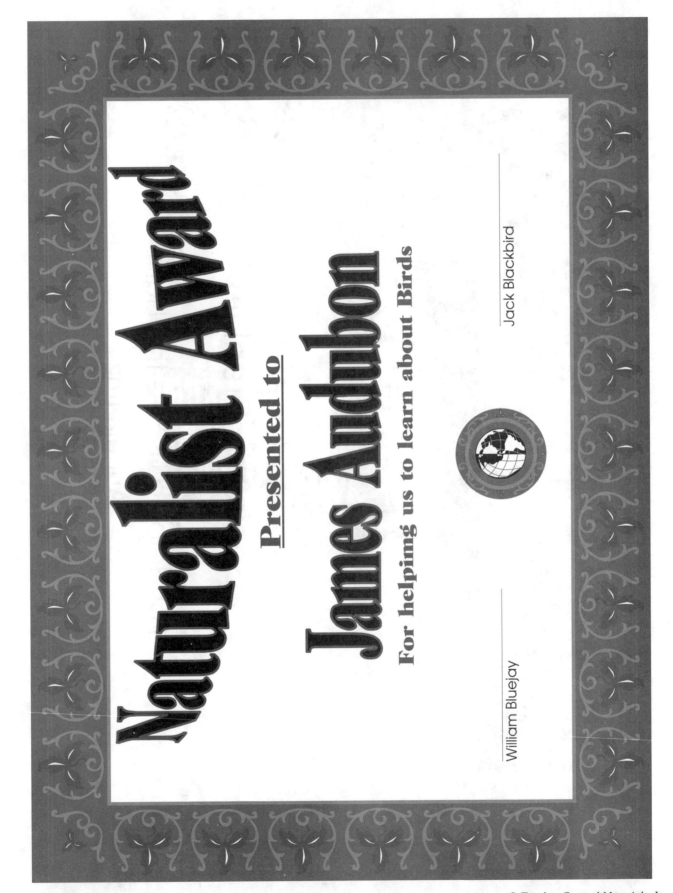

Naturalist Award

Presented to

James Audubon

For helping us to learn about Birds

William Bluejay

Jack Blackbird

Cryptogram

This Project:

Making codes to send secret messages to friends and to keep messages away from others is something that is fun to do. A simple code form is to assign numbers to letters in a word and then use the numbers to write a coded word or message. A message whose meaning is hidden is called a cryptogram. In this project you are going to make your own code and then write secret words.

1. Open Sign from the Project Menu.
2. Select Wide or Tall orientation.
3. Choose No Backdrop and on the next screen choose No Layout.
4. Select the T text box from the Tool Palette and click and drag to make a text box on the screen large enough to hold a word.
5. For this example type in the word P L A Y G R O U N D. Put two spaces between each letter by pressing the space bar twice.
6. Press Return two times to get to the next line.
7. Write a number under each letter. Don't forget to put two spaces between each number. Write the numbers one through ten under the letters.
8. Now let's write some words using these numbers. Draw a small text box on the screen. Think of a word that uses some of the letters in the word PLAYGROUND. Some examples are: gray, day, ray, yard, dog, log, run, rug.
9. Use the Shift and Line key to make a line to match each of the letters in a word you have chosen. Now press Return and write numbers to represent each letter. For example, gray would be numbers 5,6,3,4. If a number does not exist to match a letter, just tell the person solving the cryptogram to guess a letter to match.
10. Make some more text boxes on the page and add more words.
11. Add a graphic to enhance your page. Select Square Graphic from the Object menu in the Tool Palette.
12. Print your page and see if your friends can solve your cryptograms.

What Else Can I Do?

- Use other words as the base for your cryptogram. You might want to use holiday words such as Christmas, Easter, Thanksgiving, Valentine, or Halloween and choose a graphic to match the theme.
- Choose a word for your cryptogram that has a social science theme such as: Oregon Trail, Gold Rush, explorers, Hudson Bay.

P L A Y G R O U N D
1 2 3 4 5 6 7 8 9 10

___ ___ ___ ___ ___ ___ ___
4 3 6 10 6 7 8 9 10

___ ___ ___ ___ ___ ___
1 2 3 4 3 2 2

Designing State License Plates

This Project:

Each state in the United States of America has a unique license plate that it issues to be placed on moving vehicles. Each state also has a state nickname. You can find the nickname of each state listed in an almanac or encyclopedia. What is the nickname of your own state? Each state also has a state flower. What is the state flower for your state? Although there are fifty states, each state has things that are unique about it. Hawaii is known for its volcanoes and beautiful flowers and ferns. Washington is known for its apples, lush forests, and vast water areas. Decide on a state. Find out information on that state. In this project you will create a license plate for the state using of the name of the state, the state nickname, and graphics for items for which the state is known.

1. Open the Sign Project from the Project Picker.

2. Select the Wide orientation by clicking on the red arrow.

3. Choose No Backdrop and click OK.

4. On the next screen double-click on No Layout.

5. Select the Square Graphic placeholder from the Object menu in the Tool Palette. The Square Graphic appears on your screen. Click your mouse arrow on one of the handles and pull it out in order to enlarge your graphic, if you want.

6. Double-click on the Square Graphic and you see a list of graphics on the screen. Choose one of the graphics that represents something associated with the state. If you need more choices, select the Change Libraries button and look through the choices there. For this example of a California license plate, graphics for music, sun activities, tennis, parades (e.g., the Rose Bowl parade), men in business, and nature were chosen.

7. Select Headline from the Object menu in the Tool Palette. Place the headline, double-click, and type in the name of the state. To change the font, highlight the text and choose a font from the Text menu. You can change the color by highlighting the text and choosing a color from the Tool Palette.

8. Select the Text tool from the Tool Palette and click and drag to make a text box somewhere on the license plate where you can write the nickname of the state.

9. Think about the special things that make your chosen state unique. Select the Square Graphic placeholder from the Object menu and place it on your license plate. Double-click to find the graphic that represents your state. Place many graphics on the license plate so that people viewing it can identify the state easily.

10. Now make a frame for the license plate by selecting Border from the Object menu and choosing an appropriate border. Either a thick band in color or any border that depicts the state will do well.

11. Save and print your license plate.

What Else Can I Do?

- Make a personalized license plate for a friend who lives in another state and send it to them.
- Make a license plate for your grandparents with their name in place of the state name. You could import graphics that remind you of them.
- If you are doing a state report for a social studies project, create a license plate with the name of the state, the state bird, the state nickname, and the official state song name. This would be a good cover for a printed report.
- Make your teacher a personalized license plate with graphics that remind you of the teacher.

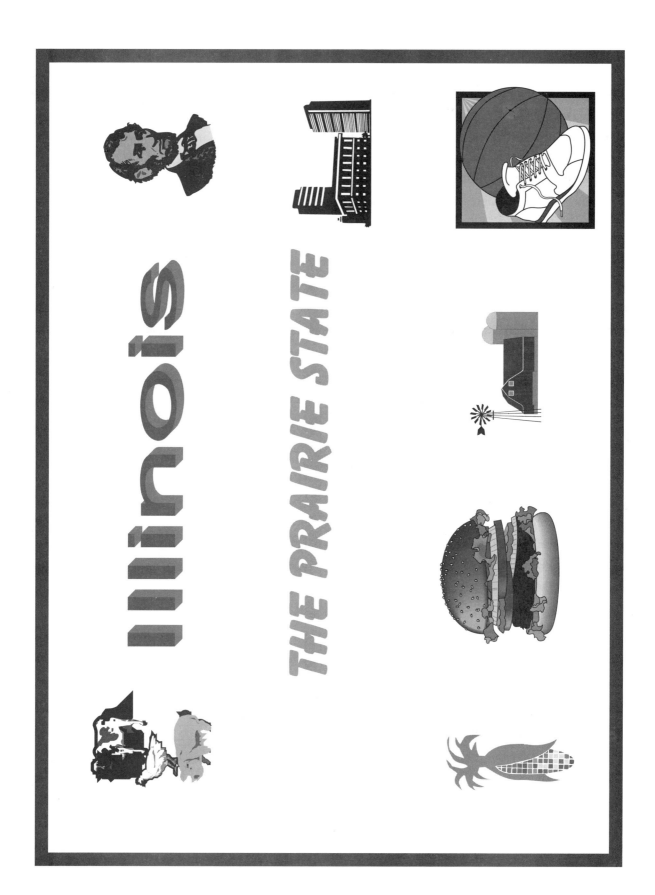

Making Greeting Cards

This Project:

There are four types of greeting cards that you can make using *The Print Shop*. Among the most popular forms of greeting cards are the side-fold and the side-fold spread. You are going to make a greeting card using the side-fold design. Think about the person to whom you are going to send the card. What are some favorite things that person likes? What do you want to tell this person?

1. Select Greeting Card from the Project Menu and then choose the Side Fold style.
2. You are then taken to a screen where a list of backdrops are listed. Look at the list of Landscape Backdrops that are available for your card. Click on the background that you want and click OK.
3. The next screen is where you choose a layout. The layout is the way that the card is designed and is for placement of graphics and text. You can also choose to have no layout and place the graphics and text where you want them. Click in the square next to Lighten Backdrop if you feel that the backdrop you chose is a little too bright. For this particular project, let's choose No Layout. Click on No Layout and click OK.

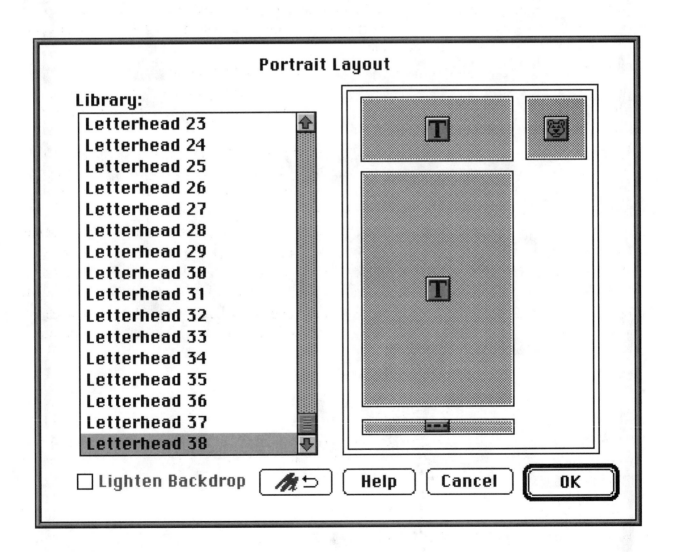

4. This next screen displays the front part of the card and is ready for you to design. Let's start by placing a picture on the front of the card.

   - Macintosh: Click on the Object icon in the Tool Palette and move your mouse to Square Graphic. On your screen a Square Graphic placeholder appears.
   - Windows: Select Graphic from the menu bar at the left side of the screen.

5. Double-click on the placeholder and a list of available graphics appears. Click on the graphic and click OK. The graphic appears on your screen. If there is not a graphic that you want, you can change libraries and search for another.

   - Macintosh: Click on the Change Library button and choose a graphic from the libraries listed. You might have to go to the desktop to find the other libraries.
   - Windows: Browse through the libraries listed on the screen.

6. After you place your graphic, you can still modify the size and placement.

   - Delete: If the handles are still around the graphic, press the delete key. To get the handles around the graphic, click once on the graphic.
   - Modify Size: Move the handles out or in to make it bigger or smaller.
   - Move: Put your mouse arrow in the center of the graphic and hold down the mouse button as you move the graphic where you want it.

   You can add as many graphics as you want following the directions given above.

7. Now write some text for the front of your greeting card. Select the text tool T from the Tool Palette. Click where you want the text and drag diagonally to the size you will need. You can always change the size later.

   Type your text in the box. If you need it larger just pull one of the handles out. You can also change font and size. Remember you must highlight what you want to change. (Highlight your text by holding down the mouse arrow at the beginning of the text and moving over the text.)

   - Font: Select Text from the menu bar. Choose Font and select a font from this list.
   - Size: Select Text from the menu bar. Choose Size and select a size from the choices presented.

8. To move to the inside of the card, select Project from the menu bar and move the mouse to Inside of Card. Choose No Layout. Now use the text and graphic tools to complete the inside of the card. To put a border around your page, select Borders from the Object menu on the Tool Palette.

9. To finish the card, select Project from the main menu and choose Back of Card. Here you can write your name in very small letters at the bottom just like the regular store bought cards show. You can also add a graphic.

   Square Graphic: Can be changed in size and location.

   Column Graphic: Places a vertical graphic on the page.

   Graphic: Places a horizontal graphic on the page.

10. Print your card. Select File and choose Print. The entire card will be printed on the page, and you can fold it into the card form. (Before folding part may be upside down.) You might have to trim the edges a little.

What Else Can I Do?

- Make birthday cards for friends and relatives.
- Create holiday cards for literary characters in the books you are reading.
- Create greeting cards as if they were being sent by historical figures.

Have a good
trip to North
America. We
will miss you all.

Smooth Sailing!

Printers of England

Good Sailing...
to the people on
the Mayflower

September 16,
1620

Making Greeting Cards *(cont.)*

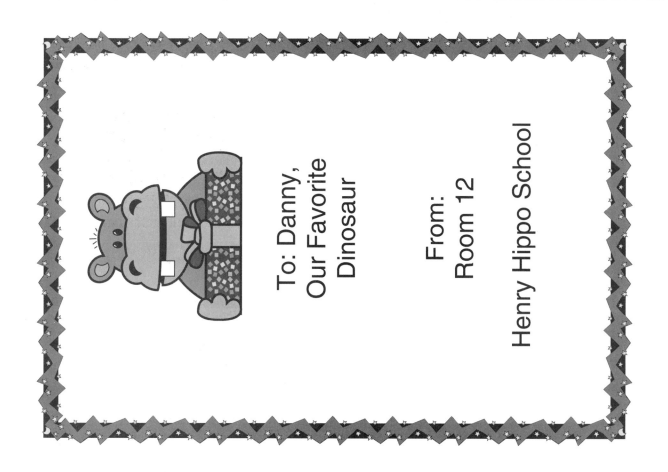

To:, Danny, Our Favorite Dinosaur

From:
Room 12

Henry Hippo School

Happy Birthday

Class Secretary
Hip, Hip, Hooray!

Holiday Prints

This Project:

You can easily make decorations for your home and room using the Print Shop Backdrops and Square Graphics. It's fun to put different designs together to create your own special print.

1. Open the Sign project from the Project Picker.

2. Choose either the Tall or Wide orientation.

3. Choose a Backdrop that matches the holiday theme you want. For this example we chose Easter Basket. Click OK.

4. Choose No Layout from the Layout screen so that you can create your own special design.

5. On your screen you should see a large Easter basket. Now let's put some items into your Easter basket.

6. Select Object from the Tool Palette and choose Square Graphic. On your screen is a selection of graphics from which to choose. Use the arrow next to the names of the choices to see all of them. When you find a graphic that would look good in your basket, click on the name and see the picture in the preview window. If that is the picture you want, click OK.

7. You might want to choose the bunny, teddy bear, chick, and egg. When the graphic appears on the screen, you can move it and resize it. Move your mouse to the center of the graphic, hold down the mouse button, and move the graphic to where you want it.

8. To change the size of the graphics, put your mouse arrow of a handle on one of the corners, hold down the mouse button, and move the handle in or out to change the size.

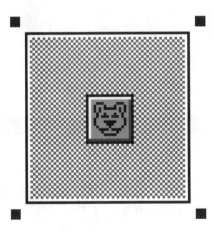

9. If you want to add text to your design, select the Text icon from the Tool Palette and click and drag to make a text box. Type in the title of your picture.

10. After you type in your text, you can change it very easily. All you need to do is to highlight your text and make the changes. Highlighting text means to put the mouse at the beginning of the word or words you want to change, hold down the mouse button, and move over the word or words. This adds a color line on the text and means that it is highlighted. Select Text from the menu bar and choose Size and Font. Make your choices, and the text that is highlighted changes.

11. To add a border to your project, select the New Object Tool from the Tool Palette and move to the word Border. A grey area surrounds the menu. Double-click on the grey border and you see a list of borders from which you can choose. Select a border from the list of borders that is shown on the screen. Click once on a border name to see it in the preview box. Double-click on the one you want or click OK. If after you placed the border you want to change it, double-click on the border and you are taken back to the border choice dialog screen.

12. To change the color of the text after you key it in, highlight the text, choose the Color Control Palette from the Tool Palette, and move the mouse to the color you want.

13. Print your creation by choosing Print from the File menu.

What Else Can I Do?

- Cut out the basket along the border and staple to a box which has been cut down. This makes a nice Easter basket for you to fill with candies and other fun things.

- Choose another theme such as Halloween and select a backdrop for it. Add square graphics to enhance your picture.

- You can make your picture into a poster by choosing a larger size when printing. Check with your teacher to see if it is Okay to print your picture in poster size.

My Easter Basket

Happy Halloween!

Making Personal Stationery

This Project:

It's fun having your own personalized stationery. You can use it to send notes to your friends and relatives. You'll need to decide on a graphic that best represents you. After you design and print your letterhead, you can have it duplicated at a store where they make copies. You can also write a note on the stationery and then print it.

1. Open Letterhead from the Project Menu.

2. The next screen lets you choose either a Single Page (8.5 x 11" letterhead size) or Notepad size (5.5 x 8.5", printed two to a sheet).

3. For this project we chose Single Page.

4. On the next screen you can choose a backdrop or a blank page on which design your layout.

5. The next screen lets you choose whether to design your own layout or use a layout that has already been designed. For this example we are using Letterhead 38. This layout gives you a place for your address and a square graphic. It also has a text area and even a place for a graphic line at the bottom. Scroll down the list and double-click on Letterhead 38.

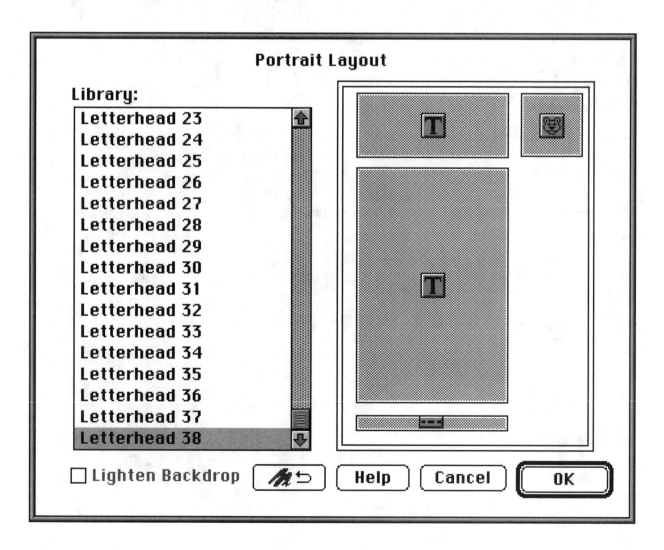

6. Double-click on the Text placeholder in the upper left-hand corner. Enter your text. Key in your information: name, street address, city, state, and zip. You can choose another font and size by selecting Text from the menu bar and then choosing size and font.

7. To add your graphic, double-click on the square graphic placeholder and choose a graphic. You might need to Change Libraries to find a graphic that suits your.

8. At the bottom of the page is a ruler line placeholder. Double-click on it and select an appropriate line design. If you do not want to use the ruled line placeholder, just click on it and press delete when the handles appear.

9. If you want to write and print a note on this page, double-click on the text placeholder and write your message. Remember you can change the size of the font, as well as the font itself, by highlighting it, and selecting Text from the menu bar.

10. If you want to make stationery to duplicate and use later, print the page you designed. When you print it the grey area of the large text box doesn't show, just a space is printed.

What Else Can I Do?

- Use some of the other layouts to create stationery for your family members as gifts.
- Design a notepad with a "making a list" theme and print it as a gift for a friend.
- Make stationery that can be used for thank you notes.
- Make stationery that could have been used by historical figures such as George and Martha Washington or Paul Bunyan and his blue ox, Babe.

Making Personal Letterhead Stationery *(cont.)*

Dear Mr & Mrs Smythe:

It was so very, very cold at Valley Forge. My troops and I were freezing. When your box of mittens arrived, it made us so happy. We look forward to spring.

G. Washington

George and Martha Washington

Dear Mr & Mrs Smythe:

It was so very, very cold at Valley Forge. My troops and I were freezing. When your box of mittens arrived, it made us so happy. We look forward to spring.

G. Washington

George and Martha Washington

Making Personal Letterhead
Stationery *(cont.)*

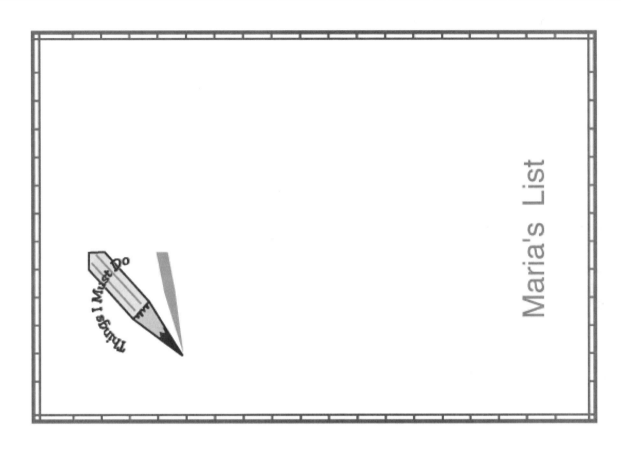

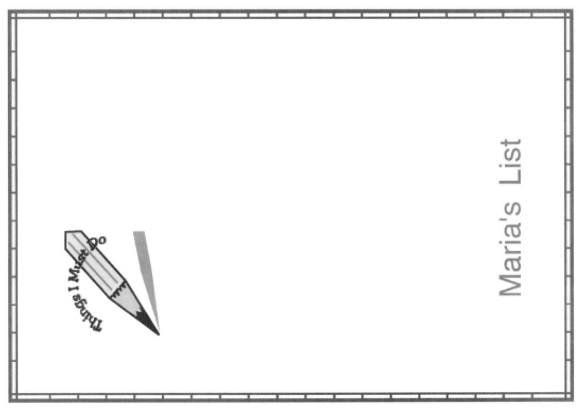

Menu Madness

This Project:

Using your imagination, you can make really creative theme menus for imaginary restaurants. Think of a theme that you can use. You might want to choose an animal theme and name the various restaurant dishes with animal names. Perhaps you want to use a space theme as is done in the example used here. Other themes might be sports, nature, literary characters, health, or Carmen San Diego.

1. Select Sign project from the Project Menu.

2. Choose a Backdrop that matches your theme. For this example we chose Space. Click OK.

3. Choose No Layout from the Layout screen so that you can create your own layout.

4. Select the Text tool from the Tool Palette. Click on the left side of the screen and drag to make a text box that is large enough to include names and descriptions of food items. Don't worry if the box is too small. Click on the arrow in the Tool Palette and click on the text box. This brings four handles around the text box. Click on one of the handles and pull it out a little. This makes the box bigger.

5. Write the names of your food creations. If you want a different font or a smaller or larger-sized font, double-click in the text box and highlight the text. Highlighting text means to put the mouse at the beginning of the word or words you want to change, hold down the mouse button, and move over the word or words. This adds a color line on the text and means that it is highlighted. Select Text from the menu bar and choose Size and Font. Make your choices and the text that is highlighted changes.

6. To add a border to your menu, select the New Object Tool from the Tool Palette and move to the word Border. A grey area surrounds the menu. Double-click on the grey border and you see a list of borders from which you can choose. Select a border from the list of borders that is shown on the screen. Click once on a border name to see it in the preview box. Double-click on the one you want or click OK. If after you placed the border you want to change it, double-click on the border and you are taken back to the border choice dialog screen.

7. To change the color of the text after you key it in, highlight the text and choose the Color Control Palette from the Tool Palette and move the mouse to the color you want.

8. Print your menu by choosing Print from the File menu.

What Else Can I Do?

- Create and print a menu with a Carmen San Diego theme. You can add some extra graphics from the Square Graphic selections. There are many Carmen San Diego choices.

- Make an animal theme menu.

    > You could have:
    > Doggy Desserts–Dog gone good doughnuts
    > Moose Muffins–Big chocolate chip delights
    > Cat Catsup–Meowingly delicious
    > Cow Crinkle Cereal–Crispy, little moovelous grains
    > Buffalo Biscuits–Large, flat, brown bread
    > Bird Berry Dessert–Blueberry sauce over beaks of ice cream

- How about a menu based on a story that you have read. Take the story of Jack and the Beanstalk and make food items based on the story. You could have giant Eggs, harp Hash, Cow Cocoa, golden goose goodies, and Magic Bean Soup.

Outer Space Cafe

Whirling Wedges Wedge shaped potatoes served on a flying saucer

Star Slurpy Makes your tongue twinkle

Moon Rocks Chocolate cookies that melt in your mouth

Sun Soda Makes you feel warm all over

Gravity Goodies Sandwiches that give you a lift

Space Sandwich Space sticks on wheat bread

Animal Alley Cafe

Doggy Desserts

Doggone good donuts

Moose Muffins

Big chocolate chip delights

Cat Catsup

Meowingly delicious

Cow Crinkle Cereal

Crispy, little moovelous grains

Buffalo Biscuits

Large, flat, brown bread

Jack's Place

Giant Eggs

Harp Hash

Cow Cocoa

Golden Goose
Goodies

Magic Bean Soup

Name Mobiles

This Project:

In this project you are going to make a mobile using the letters of your name. After you have printed the letters, you paste them together and attach a string or piece of fishing line to them. You then hang them from a decorated hanger or piece of wire as a decoration for your room.

Making the pieces that hang from the mobile:

1. Select Sign project from the Project Screen.

2. Choose the Wide orientation from the next screen.

3. Choose No Background and then No Layout from the next screen.

4. On your screen you have a wide blank page on which to create the hanging parts of your mobile.

5. Select Square Graphic from the Objects menu. Locate one of the many alphabets in the graphics libraries. Select the letter you need and place it on the screen. You need to place four letters on the top of the page and then duplicate the letters at the bottom of the screen so that both sides of the letter are decorated when printed and assembled into the mobile.

6. To duplicate your letters, click once on the letter and select Copy from the Edit menu. Click on where you want the letter to be and select Paste from the Edit menu. If the letter appears over the original letter, just hold down the mouse arrow on the letter and move it down.

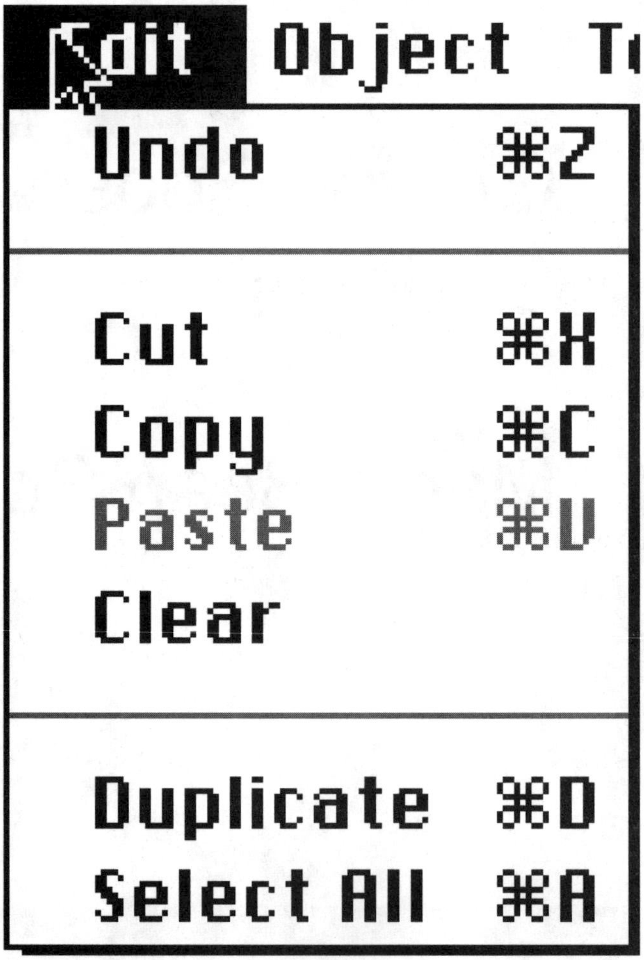

Edit	Object	Tↄ
Undo		⌘Z
Cut		⌘X
Copy		⌘C
Paste		⌘U
Clear		
Duplicate		⌘D
Select All		⌘A

7. Turn the letters at the bottom of the page around so that when you cut and paste them to the other letters they will match. This is very easy to do. Click once on the letter at the bottom, and click on the Flip Tool in the Tool Palette. Move your cursor to the word Horizontal, and the graphic turns. Do this to each of the graphics at the bottom. If your name needs more space for the letters, complete the first page and then put the rest of your letters on a new page. Save and print the first page and then create the next page.

8. Print the page. Now we will create the decoration for the front of the hanger.

Making the decorations for the top part of the mobile

1. Open the Sign project from the Project Menu and choose wide orientation.

2. Select a Square Graphic that tells something about you. Do you like sports? Are you an avid reader? Do you like to bike? You can find graphics for all of these areas of interest.

3. Now write something about you. Select the Headline placeholder from the Object menu. Double-click on the Placeholder and write in your text. To change the color of the text, choose Options from the bottom of the screen and choose a color.

4. When your graphics and text are complete, print.

Assembling the mobile

1. Cut out the letters of your name and glue an end of the string or line to the back. Glue the matching letter to the back covering the string or line. Repeat this for all of the letters.

2. Cover the hangar with paper, either colored or plain. Paste your hanger cover to the front. Hang the letters by tying the strings or wires to the bottom of the hanger.

3. Hang your mobile where everyone can enjoy it.

What Else Can I Do?

- Make a mobile with a specific theme, such as sports, using the steps outlined above.
- Make a mobile using the globe as the top and the flags of the world as the hanging pieces of the mobile.
- Make a holidays mobile.
- Make an animal mobile to give to a friend.
- Make a mobile with a family theme. Write your family name with individual letters and create a picture description of your family for the top of the mobile.

Writing a Newspaper

This Project:

Writing a class newspaper can be fun as a class project where classmates add articles of interest to the newspaper or as an individual project where one person writes the entire newspaper.

In this project you will create a class newspaper.

1. Select Sign from the Project Menu. Choose No Background. If you want to create your own layout with a masthead and 2 columns then choose No Layout and create your own. If you want to use a pre-determined layout, choose one of those listed. For this example, we used Sign 16.

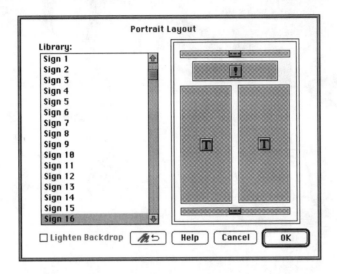

2. If you want to create your own layout, you need to choose No Layout and then add the sections that you want. You can select the Headline Block from the Object menu or from Object in the Tool Palette. You want a Headline across the top of the page for the masthead and Text Blocks for the two columns.

3. The masthead is the area where the title of the newspaper is written. Double-click on the masthead area which is the Headline placeholder and key in your title. You might also want to have a graphic in the masthead. If you want a graphic, select Object and then Square Graphic from the Tool Palette. Place the Graphic Placeholder where you want it in the masthead and use the handles to decrease the size.

4. To add ruled lines to the page, double-click on the Ruled Line placeholder and choose a ruled line that is appropriate. If you don't want the ruled lines, click on the Ruled Line placeholder and the handles appear. Now press delete.

5. To write the story, double-click in the text block. You most likely will need to choose a font size smaller than the default one. Default means that the program is set to a specific font, size, or style in this case. If you have written something and want to make it smaller or change font, then highlight the text, select Text from the menu bar, choose Size, and then a small size.

    You can also choose to justify the writing. Justify means to align the lines on the left, right, or in the center of the area. To change the justification, highlight the text and choose the new justification from the Text menu.

6. If your story is near the end of the column, double-click on the right text box and continue your story there.

7. Save and print your first page.

Writing a Newspaper *(cont.)*

Adding More Pages for the Newspaper

1. To make the second page you need only select the Sign Project and a layout that would make a good second page. You could also design the rest of the pages from scratch. Sign 14 has two columns and a masthead. If you choose this layout and don't want the masthead, click on the masthead and press delete.

2. To lengthen the columns, click on the column once and pull one of the handles upward. You can also reposition the columns by holding down your mouse button in the middle of the column and moving it.

3. You might want to add a graphic to the text area. Select Object from the Tool Palette and choose Square Graphic. Move the placeholder to where you want the graphic by holding your mouse down in the middle of the placeholder and move it to where you want it. Don't forget that you can resize the graphic by moving the handles in or out.

What Else Can I Do?

- Create newspapers as if they were published in historical times. You might create a newspaper as if it came from the time of Columbus.

- If the Pilgrims had the ability to publish newspapers, what kinds of stories would be in the papers? Write a newspaper as if the Pilgrims wrote it.

- What kind of stories would be written in a newspaper published by astronauts if they had room in their capsule to print a paper.

- Create a newspaper that tells the adventures of the pioneers on the Oregon Trail.

- Gather news from another grade, such as Kindergarten, and put it in the form of a newspaper. Imagine how thrilled that class will be to see their events in print.

Third Grade Capers

Welcome!
This is the first edition of the Third Grade Capers. This newspaper will be published every two weeks. You will read about classroom events and sports activities. There will be stories and poems written by third grade students.

Sometimes there will be games like crossword puzzles and word searches. There will also be announcements of school events. We will try to have interviews with teachers and other staff members.

Mrs. Brown is the sponsor of Third Grade Capers.

3rd Grade Performs

Room 16 played softball with Room 14 on Friday. Jane Albright pitched for Room 16 and it was a close game. There were 6 base hits and 2 homeruns by Room 16.

Jack Wells, Room 16, made the winning home run, knocking in two people. The people watching the game were very excited. Susan Smith and Tom London led the cheers.

Next week Room 16 plays Room 12.

At the Parent Teacher meeting on Wednesday night, the 3rd Grade performed "Charlotte's Web" produced by Mrs. Brown. The scenery was made in art class. The unique costumes were very hard to make and everyone had to help. The web was used as the main background and was made out of thick yarn that had been dipped in starch and sprinkled with glitter.

Each of the animals in the barnyard had speaking roles. The play announcements were made by students in the computer lab.

Third Grade Capers

Welcome!
This is the first edition of the Third Grade Capers. This newspaper will be published every two weeks. You will read about classroom events and sports activities. There will be stories and poems written by third grade students.

Sometimes there will be games like crossword puzzles and word searches. There will also be announcements of school events. We will try to have interviews with teachers and other staff members.

Mrs. Brown is the sponsor of Third Grade Capers.

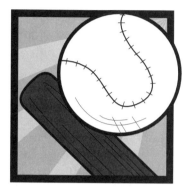

Room 16 played softball with Room 14 on Friday.
Jane Albright pitched for Room 16 and it was a close game. There were 6 base hits and 2 homeruns by Room 16.

Jack Wells, Room 16, made the winning home run, knocking in two people. The people watching the game were very excited. Susan Smith and Tom London led the cheers.

Next week Room 16 plays Room 12.

3rd Grade Performs

At the Parent Teacher meeting on Wednesday night, the 3rd Grade performed "Charlotte's Web" produced by Mrs. Brown. The scenery was made in art class. The unique costumes were very hard to make and everyone had to help. The web was used as the main background and was made out of thick yarn that had been dipped in starch and sprinkled with glitter.

Each of the animals in the barnyard had speaking roles. The play announcements were made by students in the computer lab.

Creating Advertisements

This Project:

For this project you will imagine that you have a product that you want to sell. It could be something that you have too many of or perhaps something that you don't want anymore. It could even be for a product that you create. You need to figure out what features of your product make it unique and would make it a product that someone else would want. Decide what price you should charge for your product. The price has to be set so that other people will not think it is too much. The example presented is for a new soft drink called Funky Fizz. After reading the ad, would you buy it?

1. Open the Sign Project from the Project Picker.

2. Select the Wide orientation by clicking on the red arrow.

3. Choose No Backdrop and click OK.

4. On the next screen double-click on No Layout.

5. Select the Square Graphic placeholder from the Object menu in the Tool Palette. The Square Graphic appears on your screen. Click your mouse arrow on one of the handles and pull it out in order to enlarge your graphic.

6. Double-click on the Square Graphic and you see a list of graphics on the screen. Choose one of the graphics that fits with the concept in the advertisement. If you need more choices, select the Change Libraries button and look through the choices there. For this example, aluminum cans were chosen to represent the soft drink containers.

7. To add text to the ad, select Headline from the Object menu in the Tool Palette. Place the Headline, double-click and key in the headline for the ad. To change colors, highlight the text and choose the color from the Tool Palette. Place your mouse cursor on the arrow next to the black bar under the word Text in the Tool Palette. Move your mouse to the color you want and let go. Your text changes to that color. To change fonts, highlight the text, select text from the Menu bar, and choose another size.

8. Write more text by choosing the Text tool from the Tool Palette. Click where you want the text and drag to the size you want. Type in more ad information. To place a border around the text, click on the arrow in the Tool Palette and then click on the text. Next, select the Border icon from the Tool Palette. Hold down the mouse button and move to the type of border you want. You can change the color of the border by selecting the color bar and moving to the color that you want.

9. When your ad looks like it can sell your product, select Print from the File menu.

10. Remember that if you are going to save your picture, be sure and check the box Full Save.

Creating Advertisements *(cont.)*

What Else Can I Do?

- Make an advertisement for selling Beanie Babies®.
- Make an advertisement for a unique new ice cream. How about Chicken Scratch Chocolate? It has tiny pieces of chocolate in a peanut-butter base.

Beanie Babies for Sale

SEE TOM FOR THE BEST BUYS!

Oscar Owl

Bobby Bear

SPECIAL SALE

Beanie Babies

Chippy Chicken

Potsey Polar

Holiday Place Mat

This Project:

It's very nice to have your very own place mat to use at a holiday party. In this activity you can make place mats for yourself, all of your family members, or your classroom friends. Your place mats can be as elaborate or as simple as you want to design. This example is a place mat for a Valentine's Day party.

1. Select Sign from the Project Menu screen.
2. Select No Backdrop if you want to design your own mat from scratch and click OK.
3. Select No Layout if you want to make your own placement of the graphics and text and click OK.
4. Select Square Graphic from the Object menu in the Tool Palette.
5. Place your Square Graphic placeholder where you want the graphic. Remember that you can change the placement later.
6. Double-click on the Square Graphic placeholder and choose an appropriate graphic to place on your design. You may have to click on the Change Library button or search the graphic folders to find just the correct graphic.
7. If you want to place a border around your place mat, select the Border choice from the Object menu in the Tool Palette. When you select the Border option, you are presented with a grey area on the screen. Double-click on the grey area and a list of borders appears. Click on the border that you want, and it is placed on the screen.
8. To add text to the place mat, select the Text tool from the Tool Palette and click and drag to make a text box. Key in your holiday greeting or poem.
9. Print your place mat.

What Else Can I Do?

- Print your place mat out as a small tablecloth. Choose the Print option from the File menu. At the dialog box, choose More Options and then at the Project Size box, hold down the arrow and choose 4x4. This prints your place mat at four pages across and four pages down.

- Make a place mat featuring a storybook character. How about a place mat for the three bears' picnic?

- Ask you teacher if you can print your project on heavy paper or cardstock. Your teacher might like to make a display of all the place mats on the bulletin board.

Happy Valentine's Day

Making Holiday Postcards

This Project:

A unique way to create your own special greetings is to use the Postcard project. In this project you will create a graphic scene on the front of the card, and then write your greeting on the back. When you print your creation, it prints four to a page so that you have four cards to send that are the same.

1. Open Post Card from the Project Menu and choose Wide orientation.

2. Select a Landscape Backdrop design that you want to use as your background. Click OK.

3. On the screen is your chosen backdrop. There is room for you to write a message. Select the Text tool from the Tool Palette. Click and drag diagonally to make a text box. Write your message in the text box.

4. If you need to change the font, size, or style of the text, highlight it and select Text from the menu bar. Then choose the font, size, or style that you want.

5. Let's add a border for the front of the card. Select the Object icon from the Tool Palette and choose Border. You now have a greyed-out area around the page. Double-click on the grey area and choose a border.

6. Now it is time to create the back of the postcard. Select Project from the menu bar and choose Back of Postcard. You can choose a layout from the next screen or you could choose No Layout and create your own.

7. Double-click on the Text Box placeholder and write your message. Remember that if you want to change your text, highlight the text and make changes by selecting the Text menu on the menu bar and choosing your changes.

8. Add a Square Graphic to the upper right-hand side of the postcard and select a Postmark from the graphic library. That will be the area where you place your stamp.

9. Leave space on the right-hand side of the card for you to address your postcard.

10. When you are ready to print, select Print from the File menu and print your work.

11. When you elect Print from the File menu you will then be printing the back of the card. At the dialog box be sure to check Back of Card.

12. After your postcard back comes out of the printer, turn the paper over and reinsert it into the printer so that the second side is printed. To print the front of the card, select Project and choose Front of Card. When you print, the front will print. At the print dialog box be sure to click the button next to the words, Front of Card.

    If you are using cardstock for your card, print the card on regular paper to make sure you are turning it over correctly. The card project prints four to a page with cross hairs in the center of the paper to guide you in cutting.

What Else Can I Do?

- Make postcard greetings for each of the holidays you celebrate.
- Make postcards as if you were traveling somewhere and want the people at home to know about the places you are seeing.
- Make historic postcards as if they are being sent from famous people, such as Charles Lindberg, Martha Washington, Patrick Henry, or John Henry.

68

Making Puppets

This Project:

In this project you will be making puppets that you can use as stick puppets, finger puppets, or paper bag puppets. After you have designed, printed, and placed the graphic on a stick or a paper bag, you can create a story for the puppets and act it out with a friend's help. You might also write out a story in play form or use a word processor to write a story for the puppets.

1. Select Sign from the Project menu.

2. On the next screen, select No Backdrop and click OK. You are only using the graphic so you don't need to have a background.

3. Select No Layout from the next screen and click OK.

4. Select the Object tool from the Tool Palette and move your mouse over to the words Square Graphic. A Square Graphic placeholder appears on the screen. Double-click on the placeholder and you see a listing of graphics that you can use. Click once on a graphic to see it in the Preview window on the screen. When you see one you want, double-click or click OK.

5. Choose a graphic that you think would look good as a puppet. It should be colorful and clear. If you need to view more graphics, click on the Change Libraries and choose your graphic from the libraries shown.

6. When the graphic appears on the screen, you will need to enlarge it. Click and drag on one of the handles surrounding the graphic to make it larger.

7. When the graphic is the size you need, print the graphic. Select Print from the File menu.

Making Puppets *(cont.)*

Making a Stick Puppet

1. Cut out the graphic and glue it to a popsicle stick. You also could cut a rectangle from cardboard or other heavy paper to use as a stick. Just glue your printout to the stick. You could also use a straw as the holder for your puppet.

Making a Slip-On Finger Puppet

1. To make a finger puppet, select the graphic that you want and place it on one side of the screen. Click on the graphic to select it, you will have four handles surrounding the graphic. Select Copy from the Edit menu on the menu bar. Click on the other side of the screen and select Paste from the Edit menu. If the graphic shows on top of the original graphic, put your mouse arrow in the center of it and move it to the right side of the screen.
2. To change direction on the second object, click on it to highlight. Select the Flip Tool from the Tool Palette and move to the word Horizontal. Your graphic changes direction.
3. Print your page and cut out the two objects. Place the objects back to back and glue around the edges. Slip over your finger and tell your story.

Making a Ring Type Finger Puppet

1. A ring type finger puppet is made by cutting a strip of construction paper in a rectangle that fits around your finger.
2. Glue the cutout graphic to the strip and place on your finger.

Making a Paper Bag Puppet

1. Create your graphic in the largest size possible by clicking and dragging on the handles. Caution: look carefully to see that you don't make it too big and lose the color and clearness of the graphic.
2. Print and cut out your graphic. Use a small paper bag and glue the puppet on the side so that you can move the flap and make the puppet move.

Creating Scenery for Your Puppet Show

1. Select a backdrop from the Backdrop choices and print it.
2. Secure the backdrop on heavy paper and glue it to a tongue depressor. Have a friend hold the backdrop as you use your puppet in front of it.
3. Glue the backdrop to the inside of the bottom of a box and place it on a table edge facing the audience. You can perform your show in front of the scenery box.

Let's Make a Puppet Show

This Project:

In this project you get to make puppets and scenery to put on a show for your friends or family. You first need to decide on the subject of your show and which characters you want to make. You need also to write the dialogue, what the characters will be saying to each other. Planning and writing your show before you design the graphics will make it more professional looking. When your graphics are ready, you can print them, cut them out, and attach them to popsicle sticks to make stick puppets. You can also make a backdrop against which the puppets perform.

Making the Puppets:

1. Open the Sign Project from the Project Picker.

2. Select the Wide orientation by clicking on the red arrow.

3. Choose No Backdrop and click OK.

4. On the next screen double-click on No Layout. This is the screen where you will put one of the main characters and a speech bubble in which you write the text.

5. Select the Square Graphic placeholder from the Object menu in the Tool Palette. The Square Graphic appears on your screen. Click your mouse arrow on one of the handles and pull it out in order to enlarge your graphic. You want your stick puppet to be large enough to see.

6. Double-click on the Square Graphic and you will see a list of graphics on the screen. Choose one of the graphics that fits with your storyline. If you need more choices, select the Change Libraries button and look through the choices there.

7. Now it is time to put the speech bubble on the screen. Select Square Graphic from the Object menu on the Tool Palette. Look through the list of graphics and select the Speech Bubble graphic. Place it on the right side of the screen and enlarge it so that you can write in it.

8. To write inside the speech bubble, select the Text tool from the Tool Palette. Click in the upper left-hand corner of the speech bubble and drag to fill the bubble. You will need to change the size of the font in order to write. Select Text from the menu bar and then choose size. Move the highlight to a smaller size and write your text in the text box.

9. Save your picture.

10. Repeat the steps above to create more pages with a character and a speech bubble. You might want to use a thought bubble on one of your screens for a change.

11. After you have all of your characters and speech bubbles, it is time to create the background scenery.

Making Scenery

1. Open the Sign project from the Project Picker.

2. Choose the Wide orientation.

3. From the list of Backdrops, choose one that is appropriate for your show. If there is not one that would work well, click on the Change Libraries button to search for more.

4. Print your backdrop. Ask your teacher if you can print it in poster size.

Let's Make a Puppet Show *(cont.)*

Putting Your Show Together

1. Cut out the puppets and the speech bubbles. Mount them on tongue depressors or popsicle sticks with glue.

2. Glue the scenery to a piece of heavy paper or card stock. You might want to put it in the inside of a box lid, tape it to the edge of a table, and then perform the show while kneeling below the table.

What Else Can I Do?

- Write and create the graphics for a puppet show based on a book that you or your class has read.

- Search through the graphics that are available in *The Print Shop* and find several that when put together would make a very funny puppet show. Some examples: an ant and an elephant discussing who is stronger, a baseball and a football discussing who goes farther.

or

- Create a puppet show depicting an historic event. Paul Revere and his horse could be shown on the Liberty Bell with someone ringing it.

Let's Make a Puppet Show *(cont.)*

Front

Back

Note: Have students cut out their puppets and mount them together with a tongue depressor or craft stick in between.

Finger Puppet

Making Puzzles

This Project:

Designing and making a puzzle that can be shared with friends and family is really fun to do on the computer. After you design and print your puzzle, cut it in shapes and put it into an envelope so the pieces don't get lost. You might want to make a design on the envelope that lets people know what is inside.

1. Open the Sign Project from the Project Menu.

2. Select the Wide orientation by clicking on the red arrow.

3. Double-click on a Landscape Backdrop from the list of backdrops on the next screen. For this example, we used the Dino Birthday backdrop. After you double-click, the backdrop appears on the screen. If you just want to see how the backdrops look, click on the backdrop name and the picture appears in the preview box. Keep clicking on different titles and they will appear in the preview box. Click OK when you find one you like.

4. On the next screen double-click on No Layout.

5. On the next screen where you have the backdrop, let's write a title for the puzzle. Select the Text tool from the Tool Palette by clicking once on it. Put your mouse in the upper left-hand part of the screen and click and drag diagonally to make a large rectangle. This is the text box in which you will write your title. The title starts where the cursor line is in the upper left of the box. Type in the title for your puzzle. For this example we wrote, "The Dino's Birthday Party."

6. To put a border around your picture, select the Object icon from the Tool Palette and move your mouse to the right and down to the word Border. When you choose Border, a grey border appears around your picture. This is a placeholder for a border. Double-click on the grey border and a list of borders for you to use appears on the screen.

7. Look over the list of borders. To preview them, click once on the border name and it appears in the preview box on the screen. If you like the one you see, click OK. If you want to see more, click on another border name.

8. Now you have created a puzzle. Select Print from the File menu and print your puzzle.

What Else Can I Do?

- Create and print a puzzle with a holiday theme, such as Christmas, Thanksgiving, or Halloween.
- Create a puzzle using a picture that you design. Select Sign, Blank Page, and No Layout. Then use the options in the Object menu: Square Graphic, Column Graphic, Row Graphic, and Borders.
- Make a puzzle with pictures and words that tell a story.
- Ask your teacher if you can print your puzzle on heavy paper called cardstock.

Animal Sounds

cluck, cluck

moo,moo

bubble, bubble

ribbit,ribbit

chomp, chomp

neigh

Write the ABCs Template

Open the Write the ABCs template and notice the alphabet border around the page. In the center of the screen is a box. That is where you write your alphabet. Click on the text tool T from the Tool box, click in the upper left-hand corner of the box, and drag diagonally to the lower right-hand corner of the box. This gives you an area in which to write. Now use your keyboard to type in the letters of the alphabet. Print your page.

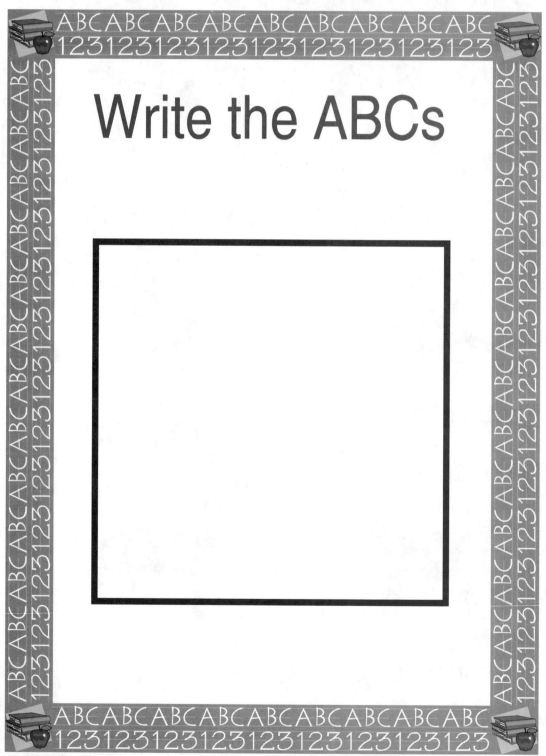

My Favorite Foods Template

Open the My Favorite Foods template and just look at all the foods that are on the screen. In the middle of the screen is a box. You can put all the foods that you like into that box.

1. Select the Graphic tool from the toolbox and move the cursor arrow to the words Square Graphic.

2. A box appears on the screen with a picture of a teddy bear in it. Double-click on the box and you will see a list of graphics to use.

3. Use the arrow at the side of the box and move it down until you see a food listed that you like. Double-click on it, and it is placed onto your screen.

4. To move it on the screen, put your mouse arrow in the middle of the picture, hold down the mouse button, and move the picture to where you want it. You can also make it bigger or smaller by putting your mouse arrow on one of the handles and holding down the mouse arrow as you move the handle in or out.

5. Print your picture.

My Favorite Foods

What's Wrong with this Burger Template

Open the What's Wrong with the Burger? template. Oh no! What has happened to this hamburger? Someone has put some weird things on it. You have to get the weird things off of the burger before someone tries to eat it. Click on one of the things that doesn't belong. You should see the graphic with four handles around it. Put your mouse arrow in the middle of the graphic and hold down your mouse button. Move the graphic to the side away from the burger. When all the weird ingredients are removed, print your hamburger. You might want to give it to a friend to eat.

What's Wrong with the Burger?

Take away the food that doesn't belong. Click on the food and move it to the edge.

Number Order Template

Open the Number Order template and look at the numbers made from animal shapes. The problem is that the numbers are not in the right order. You need to click on each number along the bottom of the page and move the number to the right place on the number line. The penguin number one is waiting for you.

Click and drag the numbers to put them in the right order.

Find the Letter Template

Open the Find the Letter template and look at all the letters. Do you see the letter K made from a man's head and beard? How much fun it is to make a U with arms high up. The surfer letter A looks ready for the beach. At the right side of the screen are pictures of the words cake, stop, and duck. Some of the letters that belong in the words are missing. You need to find the missing letter at the bottom of the screen and click and drag it to the right place. Then print your page.

My Favorite Present Template

Open the My Favorite Present template and look at all the presents on the screen. Wouldn't it be fun if all the presents were for you? Of all the presents you have gotten, which one made you the happiest? You are going to show the present on the screen.

1. Select the Graphic tool from the tool box and move the cursor arrow to the words Square Graphic.

2. A box appears on the screen with a picture of a teddy bear in it. Double-click on the box, and you will see a list of graphics to use.

3. Use the arrow at the side of the box and move it down until you see a present listed that you liked. Double-click on it, and it is placed onto your screen.

4. To move it on the screen, put your mouse arrow in the middle of the picture, hold down the mouse button, and move the picture to where you want it. You can also make it bigger or smaller by putting your mouse arrow on one of the handles and hold down the mouse arrow as you move the handle in or out.

5. Print your picture.

My Favorite Present

It made me happy.

Who Am I? Template

Open the Who Am I? template and look in the lower left-hand corner. Have you seen him before? What is his name? Have you heard a story about him before? In the box on the screen, write his name.

Click on the Text tool T from the toolbox and click in the upper left-hand corner of the box and drag diagonally to the lower right-hand corner of the box. This gives you an area in which to write. Now use your keyboard to type in the letters of the character's name. Print your page.

Who Am I?

Packing My Suitcase Template

Open the Packing My Suitcase template and look at the vacation things to take with you on a trip. Click on the things you would take to the beach and move them to the suitcase. Print your picture.

Packing my Suitcase

Put all of the things in the suitcase that you will need for a trip to the beach.

Fourth of July Template

Open the Fourth of July template and notice the border of stars and stripes. In each of the letters in the word July there is a picture of something we think of on the Fourth of July. The J has a picture of George Washington, the U has a picture of Uncle Sam, the L has a picture of the Liberty Bell, the Y has a picture of one of the Revolutionary War soldiers and the 4 has a picture of watermelon on a checkered tablecloth. In the box at the top of the page, write the words Happy Birthday. Select the Text tool T from the toolbox, click in the upper left-hand corner of the box, and drag diagonally to the lower right-hand corner of the box. This gives you an area in which to write.

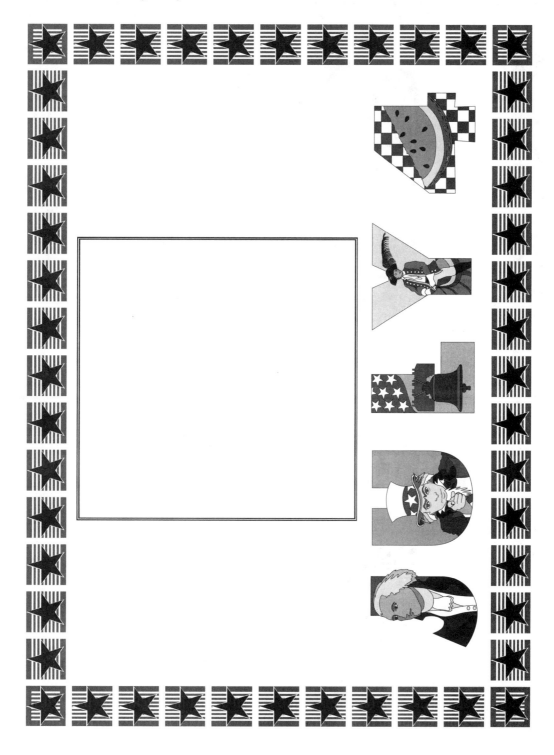

Counting by Twos Template

Open the Counting By Twos template and notice the fun Halloween numbers. Isn't the eight funny? The numbers are mixed up and you need to straighten them by putting them in order. They should read: 2, 4, 6, 8. Click on the two and move it down to the lower left-hand corner of the page. Move the four, the six, and the eight to the right places.

Click and drag
to count by twos

Label the Parts of the Bike Template

Open the Label the Parts of the Bike template and notice that there is a sketch of a bike in the middle of the screen with words pertaining to a bike listed all around the screen. Your job is to move the words to the correct location on the bike. Click on a word and, holding down the mouse button, move the word to the correct location. After you move the word, click at the edge of the screen to eliminate the handles. Print the labeled bike when you are finished.

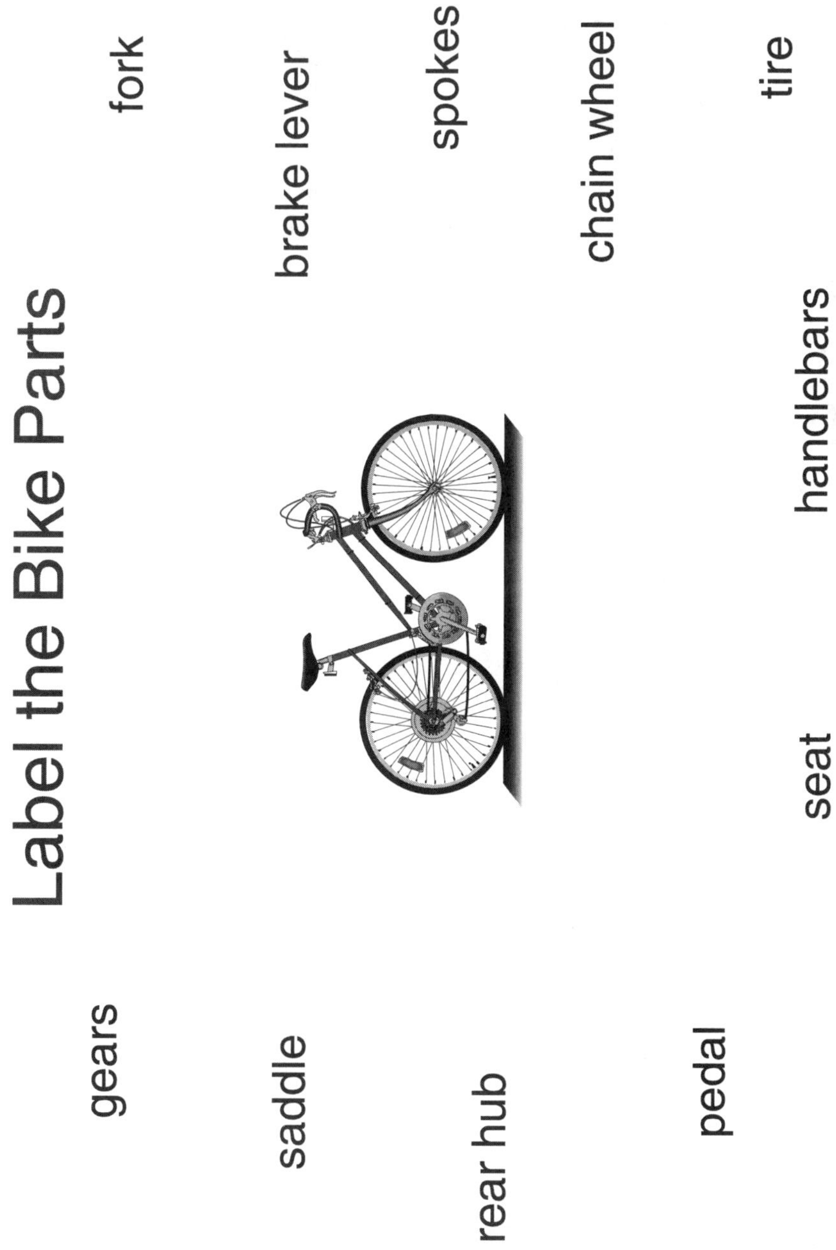

Label the Bike Parts

fork

brake lever

spokes

chain wheel

tire

handlebars

seat

gears

saddle

rear hub

pedal

Name That Flag Template

Open the Name That Flag template and note the various type of flags on the screen. You are going to put the name of the country underneath the appropriate flag. To do this you might need to use an atlas or encyclopedia as a reference. Select the Text tool from the Tool Palette, make a small text box under the flag, and then key in the name of the country.

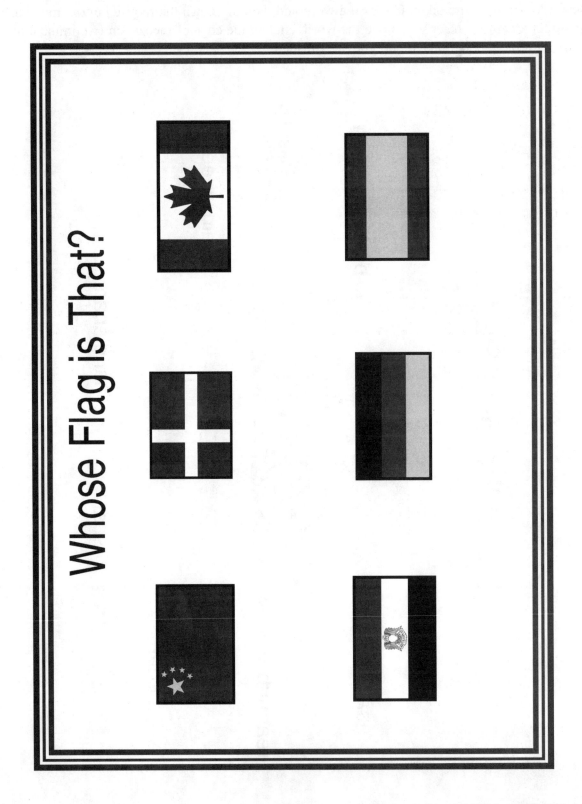

Make an Historical Certificate Template

Open the Make an Historical template and notice that the screen has a layout for a certificate for Benjamin Franklin. The name is written in for you and all you have to do is to finish the certificate. Double-click on the text box, and because the text is so small, select Text on the menu bar and choose Size and then Medium. Now key in your text telling the reason for the award. Some reasons for the award might be: organized a postal system, library, hospital, fire station, and newspapers, invented the Franklin stove, lightning rod, rocking chair, harmonica, and bifocal glasses; discovered electricity; or studied the behavior of the Gulf Stream in the Atlantic Ocean.

1. Click on the Pointer Tool and then double-click on the seal in the lower right of the screen. Double-click on the Seal Center button and choose an appropriate seal center. Next double-click on the Seal Edge button and choose an edge.

2. To choose a border, double-click on the grey border and choose a border from the list on the dialog screen.

3. Print your award certificate.

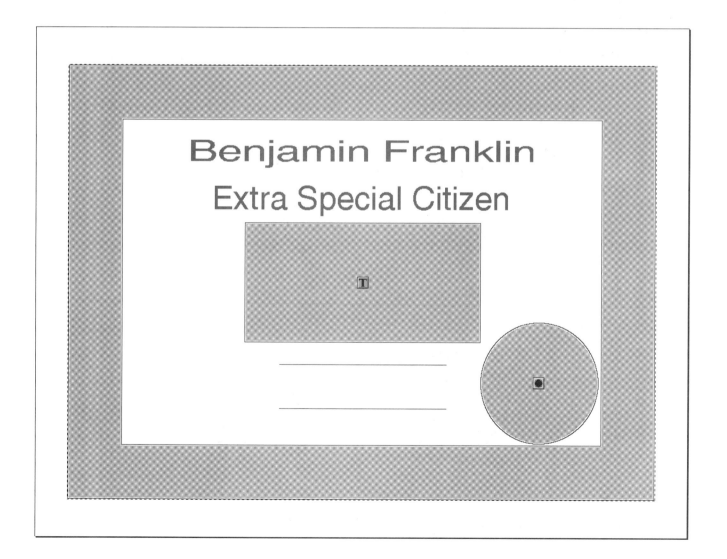

Write a Rhyme Template

Open the Write a Rhyme template and notice that there is just a part of a poem there. The last words of each line are missing. It's your job to put in the missing words. Figure out the missing rhyming word first. To key in the words, select the Text tool from the Tool Palette, click next to the last word, press the space bar once, and enter the missing word. Finish the poem by keying in all the missing words and then print the poem.

Spring

It's almost
that time of   .

When children
all through the   .

The air is warm,
the sky is   ,
the leaves are green because they're

.

So give a   ,
for spring is   .

Write a Diamante Template

Open the Write a Diamante template and notice that the poem is in the shape of a diamond. The diamante is a diamond-shaped poem with a specific format and does not usually have rhyme. The diamante's form is as follows:

> 1 noun
>
> 2 adjectives describing the first noun
>
> 3 words showing the first noun in action
>
> 4 words that show a connection between the two nouns
>
> 3 words showing the final noun in action
>
> 2 adjectives describing the final noun
>
> 1 noun

1. Read the diamante and add the missing words. Click next to the preceding word and type in the missing word.
2. Print your diamante.

Bee
Tiny,
Buzzing,   ,
Animal,   , eats,
Running,   ,
Enormous,
Elephant

On Halloween Template

Open the On Halloween template and look at all the bats flying around the edges of the screen. In the middle of the page is a box where you can write what you want to be for Halloween. Click on the Text tool T from the toolbox. Click in the upper left-hand corner of the box and drag diagonally to the lower right-hand corner of the box. This gives you an area in which to write.

You many need to change the size of the print in order to get all your words into the text box. To change the size of the text, select the Text menu from the menu bar and move your mouse to a smaller size that is shown to the right. Key in your text.

You can change the text color and size after you key it in. Highlight the text by holding down the mouse arrow and moving over the text. Now use the Text menu to change your print. When you are finished, select Print from the File menu and print your Halloween story.

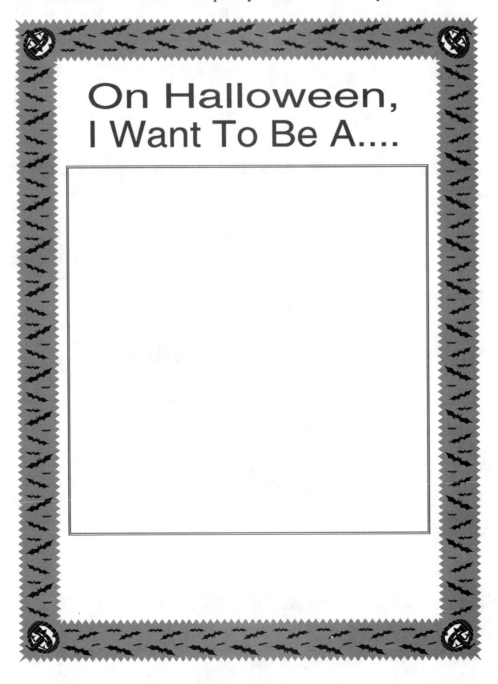

Make a Funny Pizza Template

Open the Make a Funny Pizza template and look at the pizza. Oops, at the bottom of the page are some interesting foods and a bee, too.

Look over the pictures at the bottom of the page. Click on a picture of something that you want to add to your pizza. Notice the handles that appear around the picture. Put your mouse arrow in the middle of the picture and, holding down your mouse button, move the picture to the pizza.

Make it taste really good. Select Print from the File menu and print your pizza when you are finished. Do you think it will taste good? Hmmmm!

CD-ROM Filenames

Examples

Macintosh Filename	Windows Filename	Macintosh Filename	Windows Filename
3 Bears Placemat	3BEARMAT.PDS	Jessie James Greeting Card	JESSEJMS.PDG
Animal Menu	ANIMAL.PDS	John's Banner	JOHNS.PDB
Animal Sounds Puzzle	ANIMSNDS.PDS	Letterhead	LETTERHD.PDS
Audubon Certificate	AUDUBON.PDS	Lopez Family Mobile	LOPEZFAM.PDS
Basketball Puzzle	BASKETBL.PDS	Lopez Family Mobile 2	LOPEZFM2.PDS
Beanie Babies	BEANBBYS.PDS	Mayflower Greeting Card	MAYFLOWR.PDG
Ben Franklin Certificate	BENFRANK.PCC	Moose and Mice Alliteration	MOOSE.PDS
Book Report Banner	BOOKREPT.PDB	Newspaper 1	NWSPAPR1.PDS
Butterfly Finger Puppet	BUTTRFLY.PDS	Newspaper 2	NWSPAPR2.PDS
California License Plate	CALIFRNA.PDS	October Calendar	OCTOBER.PDC
Carmen Menu	CARMEN.PDS	Panda Alliteration	PANDA.PDS
Columbus Day Banner	COLUMBUS.PDB	Playground Crptogram	PLAYGRND.PDS
Dinosaur Greeting Card	DINOSAUR.PDG	Sally Ride Certificate	SALYRIDE.PDS
Duck Stick Puppet	DUCK.PDS	Smooth Sailing	SMOOTHSL.PDG
Easter Basket	EASTER.PDS	Solve It!	SOLVEIT.PDS
February Calendar	FEBRUARY.PDC	Space Menu	SPACE.PDS
Flash Cards	FLASHCRD.PDS	Sports Mobile	SPORTS.PDS
Funky Fizz	FUNKYFIZ.PDS	Sports Mobile 2	SPORTS2.PDS
G. Washington Note	WASHNGTN.PDS	Things to Do Notepad	THNGTODO.PDS
Good Luck Greeting Card	GOODLUCK.PDG	Turkey Puppet	TURKEY.PDS
Halloween Placemat	HALOWNMT.PDS	Valentine's Placemat	VALENMAT.PDS
Halloween Placemat 2	HALOWMT2.PDS	Weekly Calendar	WEEKLY.PDC
Holiday Postcard	HOLIDAY.PDS	World Mobile	WORLD.PDS
Illinois License Plate	ILLINOIS.PDS	World Mobile 2	WORLD2.PDS
Jack's Place Menu	JACKSPLC.PDS	Year 2000 Calendar	YEAR2000.PDC

Template Activities

Macintosh Filename	Windows Filename	Macintosh Filename	Windows Filename
ABCs Template	ABCS.PDS	Number Order Template	NUMORDER.PDS
Ben Franklin Template	FRANKLIN.PDS	Packing Suitcase Template	SUITCASE.PDS
Burger Template	BURGER.PDS	Pizza Template	PIZZA.PDS
Counting by 2s Template	COUNT2S.PDS	Present Template	PRESENT.PDS
Dino's Birthday Puzzle	DINOBDAY.PDS	Spring Template	SPRING.PDS
Find the Letter Template	FINDLETR.PDS	USA Template	USA.PDS
Flags Template	FLAGS.PDS	Who Am I Template	WHOAMI.PDS
Foods Template	FOODS.PDS	Write a Diamante Template	DIAMANTE.PDS
Halloween Template	HALLOWEN.PDS	Write a Rhyme Template	RHYME.PDS
Label Bike Parts Template	BIKEPART.PDS		